THE SERPENT

Birgitte Rasine's *The Serpent and the Jaguar* stands out among the plethora of recent books on Mayan calendars by offering us a profoundly practical approach to the Tzolk'in, guiding readers in applying the wisdom of the ancient "count of suns" to their own daily lives. She gracefully avoids the hype and self-serving tendencies that infect the 2012 phenomenon, and instead inspires us to reflect upon ourselves in ways that our fast-paced modern lifestyle rarely allows.

— Robert Sitler, PhD
Director, Latin American Studies, Stetson University

Beginning with the ground-laying Foreword by Kenneth Johnson, to the process for accessing personal guidance described by the author, Birgitte Rasine, to the poetic daily rendering of the Tzolk'in calendar, this book is far and away the most accessible and spiritually commanding work of its genre. *The Serpent and the Jaguar* is a must read, and one to be practiced faithfully—above all for understanding the cyclical nature of the Maya way that guides our own path for consistently living a fruitful life in any era, at any time, from day to day. Indeed, this work of art is a measure and celebration of sacred time. The wisdom it contains is abundant and precise, the language pragmatic yet liltingly poetic, its comforting and uplifting nature unparalleled. *The Serpent and the Jaguar* belongs in every collection dealing with the Maya culture.

— Jim Young, PhD
Author and editor, *2013! The Beginning is Here*

Birgitte Rasine's intuitive and my hard-science approach may produce fundamentally different world views of the Mayan Calendar, but with this book, I get the feeling that Birgitte is just like me, trying to capture the attention of the seekers of sacred time. She wishes to lead them to deeper insights, rather than offering stimulating, or comfortable, lies. My own works have a similar aim ... Some readers may reject my message and move on, but others respond to something, something that will entice them closer to the Real Maya, ancient and modern... the farmers, poets, weavers and kings, the warriors, captives, charlatans and sages that populate the lively world that Birgitte and I love.

— Mark Van Stone, PhD
Professor of Art History, Southwestern College

The Serpent and the Jaguar invites us to step outside our Western concept of time being linear and mechanical. Instead the reader enters the world of the ancient Maya where time is a sacred natural rhythm, organic in nature and deeply personal. Birgitte's ability to elegantly explain the unique energies of the Tzolk'in calendar opens the door for just about anyone to walk through to see their world differently. Once one has crossed this threshold and entered sacred time they will truly never see their world in the same way.

This is a blessing for us as it helps us to better navigate in our modern era which is so often dominated by technology and demanding schedules.

— Michael Shore
MayanMajix.com

A very easy, practical and well organized way to understand and follow the Tzolk'in. I personally prefer a more shamanistic approach to the calendar, but in that case it may not be a book for everyone... Birgitte has simplified and made the Tzolk'in's spirituality accessible enough so that people of all mindsets can understand, especially on a basic level, the essence of the Tzolk'in.

The book is enjoyable and poetic just like the author herself.

— Lila Goldner
Sculptor
Belgrade, Serbia

Birgitte Rasine's gentle approach to understanding the numbers and [day] signs is appealing. This is a different approach, with a daily message. I like it! I would definitely buy *The Serpent and the Jaguar* to keep with my other books—I love to reference material like this.

— Anne Kessler
Dayton, Ohio

The Serpent and the Jaguar is full of energy, inspiration and wisdom—we had a lot of "God's showers" while reading it.

This is the way we have always tried to get connected with the energies of the Tzolk'in, to greet each day and honour it and to create life as artists and weavers of time. Everything is described very clearly (I personally always had problems really to understand the numbers, but this has now become clearer...) We like the way Birgitte describes the trecenas and the energies; there is a lot of information we never knew before (for example, the female and male aspects of numbers and day signs).

We hope that many, many people will read this book and follow the rhythms of sacred time!

— Martina Schröder and Wolfgang Krois
Composers and recording artists, Balanza
Germany

Love the book, love what the author has done, the writings are lovely, clear, to the point. I found when I was reading *The Serpent and the Jaguar*, I wasn't getting lost or needed to re-read that bit again. Birgitte has the flow of energy and sound coming through. When I first started to look at the Mayan calendar it all seemed strange but I fell in love with the idea that each day has its own special energy. A day was no longer just a day and if something special happened on that day then there was something to celebrate... each day [has] become a miracle, a chance to flow with my environment on a larger scale than I thought possible. It has allowed my soul to fly with the day.

— Maree Gifkins
Painter
New Zealand

Birgitte Rasine shows us in *The Serpent and the Jaguar* that the Mayan Tzolk'in Calendar is not only an age-old system for measuring time, but also a guide for one's daily life, still in use in a very real way among the Maya of today and increasingly followed by non-Mayan people.

The important message Birgitte brings is that it's not about the same energy repeating every 20 days, or the same influence of a number every 13 days, as some authors believe—the point is there are really 260 distinct energy combinations, giving each day its "unique flavor, intention, and meaning," intertwined with the spiritual world.

The Tzolk'in is both a sacred path and a highly practical instrument, helping us to live daily life in the best possible way for our needs. I see it as Birgitte's great merit that she illustrates all 260 energies of the Tzolk'in for the first time in this way. She takes us on a journey through the 260 days, showing us the ruling energies and the recommendations for each day. She lets us feel the rhythms and gives us a new point of view for our own daily lives.

Birgitte helps the reader find his or her own approach to the Tzolk'in, without using any "formulas" or "rules." And for those who may shrink from such an unfamiliar path, she offers the possibility to dip into it simply with the energy of "today." So we can all find our own personal pathway into the Tzolk'in in freedom and with our own responsibility, which will enrich our daily life in an incredible way.

— Susi Lötscher
Cultural Anthropologist
Switzerland

Birgitte Rasine delivers a wonderful exploration of the Mayan Tzolk'in calendar and sacred time. Her book is both informative and intriguing, providing thoughtful explanations of the technical and spiritual aspects of the calendar while compelling us to read more.

— Sanjay Nambiar
Author, "Maybe (A Little Zen for Little Ones)"
Los Angeles, California

The Serpent and the Jaguar is a gem. Birgitte Rasine writes beautifully and combines powerful intuition with years of scholarship and research to create what I find to be one of the most compelling books ever written about the Sacred Mayan Calendar.

— Anne-Marie van Dijk
Model and Founder of CLEANSE: one body, one planet
Paris and New York

I've proofread work from writer friends of mine and normally make LOTS of comments. With The Serpent and the Jaguar, I have only comments on the side along the lines of "well written," "wow," "wow wow wow." There is not one thing I'd put differently. This is more poetry to me than anything else. Poetry has rules of its own, and Birgitte is the master of those rules... and the result is beautiful!

It was a true honor being able to see this manuscript before it was born [as] a printed book. I feel privileged. I think Birgitte did a really good job. Not just writing-wise, but also in the fact that she put a lot of extra value to this planet by making this knowledge available. Chapeau!

— Hajo Theunissen
The Netherlands

Familiarizing oneself with the sacred energies of the Tzolk'in undoubtedly amplifies awareness. Birgitte's quest to relate the vast intricacies of the Tzolk'in will enrich many with a greater understanding of the rhythms of natural time.

— Steve Copeland
Producer and Director, "Shift of the Ages"
Los Angeles, California

THE SERPENT
AND
THE JAGUAR

Other works by Birgitte Rasine

NON FICTION

Tsunami: Images of Resilience

(coming December 2014)

FICTION

The Visionary
(coming Fall 2014)

The Origins: Chocolate
(coming December 2014)

Verse in Arabic

Confession

Bakaly

The Seventh Crane

MOBILE APPS

MCP Mayan Tzolkin

My Mayan Match

THE SERPENT
AND
THE JAGUAR

LIVING IN SACRED TIME

BIRGITTE RASINE

LUCITÀ
PUBLISHING

Published in the United States by
LUCITÀ Publishing, an imprint of LUCITÀ Inc.
Sunnyvale, California
http://publishing.lucita.net

ISBN-10: 0-9774035-2-1
ISBN-13: 978-0-9774035-2-3

Library of Congress Control Number: 2011962445

First LUCITÀ Publishing edition 2011.
LUCITÀ and the sun logo are trademarks of LUCITÀ, Inc.

Cover and book design by Luba Rasine-Ortoleva

Trecena illustrations by Maree Gifkins (reproduced in black & white)

Interior graphics by Luba Rasine-Ortoleva

The Maya day sign and number glyphs in this book are based on actual Maya carvings. The graphics have been styled for high quality printing by Luba Rasine-Ortoleva.

Visit *www.birgitterasine.com* for more information about Birgitte Rasine and her work.

Printed in the United States of America on FSC-certified, 30% post consumer recycled paper.

To my sweet beloved Aria Luna
innocence personified

CONTENTS

ACKNOWLEDGMENTS

No book is ever written alone. They say writers create in solitude—and we do—but the process of writing and producing a book is, at the end of the day, a collaborative effort. This is especially true of non fiction books, which need to be thoroughly researched, and still more so of books about topics such as the Mayan Calendar, a complex universe of cultural, historical, and societal constructs and concepts underlying a stunningly simple yet profound system of timekeeping, as often misunderstood and misrepresented as Time itself.

My thanks and gratitude to all of the peoples of Mesoamerica, ancient and living, past and present, from the Olmecs to the Maya, who have created, developed, and ensured the survival of this wondrous calendar through systematic attempts at destruction, suppression, and invalidation; through misunderstanding, misinterpretation, and misrepresentation; and through the toughest test of all, the very thing that it measures: time. Thank you, to those of you who are the Elders of humanity, from us, your children.

My personal thanks and gratitude go to the people who have made this book possible:

To Aria Luna, whose innocence, joy, and beauty of simply being herself transcend the invented ambitions of society, as they do in babies and young children, and who inspired me every day I dedicated to this book;

To Andrés, who inspired, questioned, explored, and challenged me to give more than the best of myself to every aspect of this project, and without whose full and loving support this book would never exist;

To Luba Rasine-Ortoleva, who has always been one of my biggest cheerleaders and a talented and wonderful artist whose work graces the cover of this book, and to Maree Gifkins, another outstanding artist whose work illustrates the trecenas;

To Mayan scholar and author Ken Johnson, whose limitless generosity of spirit and wealth of knowledge about the world and history of the Maya have greatly enriched my understanding of and familiarity with the use and purpose of the sacred Tzolk'in calendar and the culture that has brought it to modern society, and to whom I owe the greatest debt of gratitude in learning how to work with the calendar;

To Don Rigoberto Itzep Chanchavac, a Maya Daykeeper and the Spiritual Guide and Community Needs Advisor (in Spanish, "El Guía Espiritual Consejero Orientador de Muchas Necesidades de la Comunidad") of Momostenango, Guatemala, whose great personal warmth and grandfatherly talks have opened up for me the world of the real living Maya, and who has patiently answered all of my questions about the complexities of the Tzolk'in, or Ch'ol Q'ij as his people the K'iche' Maya call it, and to Don Gregorio, Don Rigoberto's son, who has graciously helped shepherd electronic communications between us;

To my team at the Mayan Calendar Portal, who have dedicated thousands of hours to build and support an extraordinary site and platform for exchange and dissemination of information about the sacred Mayan Calendar;

To Robert Sitler, Mark Van Stone, Anne-Marie van Dijk, John Payne, Michael Shore, and many, many others who have supported and encouraged me in my quest to know the Tzolk'in;

To all those of you who are members of the vast Mayan Calendar Portal community, encouraging our work and evolution with your enthusiasm, support and suggestions throughout the past several years. Without you there would be no Mayan Calendar Portal, and no inspiration to write this book.

Birgitte Rasine
On 1 Ix / I'x
Northern California

FOREWORD

Many of us in the Western world have come to see the Mayan Tzolk'in calendar as an astonishingly technical piece of "ancient science." A cultural artifact to be taken with the utmost seriousness, it is perceived as something to ponder deeply, with furrowed brow, in an attitude of wonderment seasoned with a touch of apocalypse.

Consequently, some may find it unusual to see the "count of days" as Birgitte Rasine approaches it—in the spirit of poetry, sometimes lyrical, sometimes whimsical, even humorous.

And yet, Birgitte's approach is more Mayan in spirit. Although it is indeed true that the ancient calendar of Mesoamerica is one of the world's mathematical marvels, it is much more than that. The Tzolk'in is the rhythm of sacred time. Anyone who has lived among those of the Maya who still keep the count of days will know that its purposes are ritual and magical rather than merely a measure of ordinary, secular time. As such, it is natural to approach the Tzolk'in in the spirit of poetry, with its infinite range of verbal music and its magic intonations, rather than in the spirit of "scientific reason" or any other Western (and hopelessly non-Maya) mental construct.

And it is in fact through poetry that the Maya express their unity with that eternal rhythmic dreamtime which is the Tzolk'in. By "dreamtime," I mean "time which is outside of time," time which obeys different tides, seasons, and circumstances than the ordinary, working-day round of the week, the month, or the year. The *Popol Vuh*, the sacred book of the Maya, tells us that the gods gave human beings a voice specifically so that they might cry out and sing of the beauty of this world, and so that they might "keep the days."

While "keeping the days" might seem, at least to some sensibilities, quite far removed from praising the beauty of this world, a traditional Daykeeper would see the act of praise and the rhythm of the Tzolk'in as closely allied. In contrast to those who see the salvation of the world in the primacy of images over the "tyranny of the word," the Maya insist that the beauty of words renders life itself more beautiful. Whenever a shaman counts the days of the Tzolk'in, each day is lovingly addressed as if it were a real entity, a living being; each day is greeted with eloquent words that describe its qualities and reach deep into the heart of ancestral myth. And so they are greeted in Birgitte's work.

Every shaman is a prayer-maker, and every prayer-maker a poet. To address the days through poetic utterance is to approach them in the spirit that the *Popol Vuh* intended. To sing the magic of the days is to enter the myth, the eternal dream which is the rhythm of sacred time. To sing the beauty and the magic of the 260 days is to use our human voices for their intended purpose—the praise of the world.

But the keeping of the days neither ignores "ordinary" time nor stands in contradiction to it. On the contrary, the Tzolk'in is just as much a guide to practical daily life as it is a spiritual path. On Lamat days, for example, one visits one's cornfield, for Lamat represents the greening of the world. Families discuss marriage plans on Akb'al days, for Akb'al is the day of romance par excellence, though the actual marriage ceremony may well be held upon a Chuen day. Men days, on the other hand, are favored for business transactions.

Like all of the world's great symbolic languages, the Tzolk'in has a universality that transcends any specific cultural context or environment; and it is here that Birgitte focuses much of her attention—upon the ways in which this ancient calendar illuminates our modern lifestyle and casts light upon our daily actions. The Tzolk'in is not an artifact to be pondered; as Birgitte asserts throughout these pages, it is an eminently practical rhythm that is to be actively lived.

Set aside your ponderous notions of ancient science. Let yourself fly and dream with these words. Enter into their spirit, the spirit of sacred time. And by all means, enjoy it.

Kenneth Johnson
On 2 Akb'al / Aq'ab'al
Santa Fe, New Mexico

AN INTRODUCTION
TO SACRED TIME

The Maya *ajq'ijab'*, or Daykeepers, the spiritual masters who keep the count of days, say it takes several rounds of studying the Tzolk'in to become sufficiently acquainted with the calendar to live your life by it, and many years to become a Daykeeper yourself. There are plenty of seminars and workshops advertised that promise to make you a Maya Daykeeper in two weeks or so, but unless you spend the time and do the work that it takes to understand and respect this ancient calendar, you're wasting your money—and cheating yourself out of the profound guidance and knowledge the Tzolk'in has to offer.

Many of us may never have the time or money to travel to Central America to study with the Maya. But that doesn't mean we cannot bring the Tzolk'in into our lives or align our lifepaths with its energies. There is nothing to keep any of us from learning about the calendar, how it works, and living with it on a daily basis—except time itself. In fact, most genuine Daykeepers would welcome such a personal study of the calendar—those who insist there is only one proper way to count the days, or that only Daykeepers are allowed to run Mayan birth charts or readings, are misrepresenting the *ajq'ij* community. Anyone can study and live with the Calendar.

Like any other important change we wish to integrate into our lives, whether it's eating healthier, sleeping or laughing more, or breaking bad habits, living with the Tzolk'in takes time, commitment, and practice. But it's more than a lifestyle change. It's a shift in your relationship with and understanding of time itself.

Everything we do and the way we think is based on a linear conception of time. Our very ideas of life, success, and happiness are tied to a non-cyclical, non-organic paradigm that often works against our own nature and essence. Instead of embodying and integrating the first cycle of our existence (that period of time we call childhood) into the next cycle, then the next one after that, and so on as we grow and evolve, we are vehemently taught by all of the major pillars of our society to "grow up" and forget all the silly things we thought and did as babies and children, and then to further "mature" and forget all the wild and crazy things we did as teenagers and as young adults. We are told both explicitly as well as through powerful subliminal messages, that we need to hit certain milestones by certain ages. One after the other, and ideally in a certain order pre-approved by society at large, or close to it: college, career, marriage, kids, home ownership, retirement.

Are we really supposed to wait till we're old to do the things we've always dreamed of? Why not start as soon as we're conscious of our dreams? And who cares in what order we live our lives?

No wonder by the time we reach our fourties and fifties, we feel empty. We have "mid-life crises" and spend a great deal of our savings on psychotherapists, anti-ageing products, self-help and self-healing books, or all of the aforementioned combined. This is the result of a linear societal mindset.

Our economy, in turn, mirrors our society: most of the products we use are designed with obsolescence in mind, so that we are obliged to buy more in the near future. The supply chain and the factory-line manufacturing process, both born of the Industrial Revolution, have traditionally followed the linear approach of extracting natural resources, manipulating and modifying them to create the product, marketing the product, the product then going through a certain lifespan in the hands of the consumer, and almost invariably ending up in a landfill or any number of what our economy considers to be lovely wastebaskets: rivers, oceans, forests, the atmosphere, and so on. It's linear: from one step to the next, from one phase to the next, until the end is reached. All in the name of progress and innovation. Only recently has manufacturing begun to experience a fundamental shift from this linear "cradle-to-grave" approach to a brilliant concept called "cradle-to-cradle," originally championed by Michael Braungart and William McDonough, which utilizes a cyclical paradigm to bring products into being and then re-purposing all of their ingredients for other uses or other products—a concept that Nature herself has been employing since the first plants started up chlorophyll production.

In fact, all of nature is cyclical. Our planet itself is not a rectangle, a box, or a line; it's a sphere. Its orbit around the sun is cyclical. Weather patterns, seasonal changes, the movement of water and air systems, the reproductive cycles and evolution of species—even the histories of human societies and cultures—are cyclical. Perhaps most ironically, the astronomical and celestial phenomena we use to measure time are cyclical, yet our definition and use of time is linear.

Simply put, linear time does not take into consideration the sanctity of Life as a whole. It places humankind at the top of a pyramid of priorities, effectively rendering all other living things and all natural systems mere resources to be used up, servants providing various services to humanity. This not only destroys our environment, drives our fellow living beings—and some of us—to extinction, and robs our children of a vibrant experience of life; it denies all of us the far greater and far more significant role as stewards of our planet and neighbors to other living species.

Despite what the marketing and media machines tell us, things like fame, wealth, and power are neither the true aspirations for life that certain parties want you to believe they are, nor do they deliver that deep, lifelong joy and happiness we all seek. If we ride that train, we're really missing out on the grandest, most magical experience of them all: living in sacred time.

This is not to suggest, of course, that everything linear is bad. There are plenty of needs for linearity in our world: we need to drive in a straight line, or at least follow the road, lest we start causing accidents or never reach our destination. Cyclical driving, so far, works only on closed courses. Business and financial transactions are generally linear, if two-way: I buy something from you, you receive money or something of equal value from me. And where would we be without linear communications? Imagine cyclical emails!

In fact, the line itself is part of sacred geometry, and one of the conceptual foundations of art, music, mathematics, and literature, perhaps the greatest gifts of humanity of all time. It connects and it leverages, it strengthens and it leads. But when applied to time, the line cuts through its inherently cyclical and organic essence, rendering it lifeless and rigid, denying its full potential, disrespecting its power and sanctity—in short, a linear expression of time mutates the very nature and experience of time.

At the end of the day, all you really need to do to make a line into a circle, is bend it and fuse the ends. So let's bend our relationship with time a little. Let's imagine what living in cyclical time could be like, how that would change our perception and experience of life, what impact it would have on our friends and loved ones. How can we achieve such a thing in the midst of the complex lifestyles so many of us lead and the fast-paced societies we live in? Where do we even begin?

First, no need to sell off all your worldly possessions and buy a plot of land in a commune or marry into a Mayan village. Like the Maya, we can live with both concepts of time, the ordinary and the sacred, the linear and the cyclical. We can continue driving along roads in a straight line even as we consider possible ways to drive less and walk more, preserving the natural resource cycles our children depend on for their future. We can continue to follow our career goals or professional ambitions even while we retain the warmth, innocence, and joy of our childhood.

When I was a child growing up in the Czech Republic, my earliest thoughts and memories were of nature. I remember laying in the grass, looking up at the sky, feeling quite sure that the clouds passing overhead were caused by the earth's rotation. I explained the concept of God to my little friends, telling them people from long ago invented God because they didn't know where thunderstorms really came from. And I climbed every tree I could find, trying out different branches so I could see what the world looked like from different "altitudes."

But what impacted me most of all was the *feeling* of time. It was ancient, eternal time, time that had existed long before I was born, time that had pulsed from past millennia through to my lifetime. This time felt different from the busy schedules all the adults seemed to be rushing around for. It was peaceful, soothing, timeless. It felt like what time *should* feel like. This was sacred time.

As I write these words, on a sunlit late October afternoon in a park in Northern California, I feel that same ancient, sacred time. It's quiet here because the usual crowds who come to this park to play soccer and volleyball, bring their children to play after school, or come for a run after work with their dogs, haven't yet arrived. Strangely, I felt this same ancient time on a small boat in the savannah of Colombia some years ago on a fishing trip, gliding down a river that has been cutting its banks much longer than any human civilization has ever survived, massive fallen palm trees submerged in its murky waters teeming with species of fish that missed the call of evolution.

I wonder if you need this silence and tranquility to feel time, especially sacred time. Perhaps so—our daily lives are full of deadlines, errands, responsibilities, layered atop a bottomless soup of electronic chatter, music, television, radio, and other devices we haven't invented yet. No wonder we spend most of our waking consciousness in ordinary time. Sacred, cyclical time is always everywhere, all around us, but we're too busy to notice it—much less enjoy it.

No matter how many years pass, how much technology we invent, how many products we manufacture, or how much knowledge and skill we amass, sacred time does not change. It's the same time the Olmecs, Toltecs, Maya, and other ancient cultures around the world knew. It's the same time babies and children feel, before we teach them how to become adults. Instead of honoring their—and our—sacred time, we deny it, cut it short.

The latest studies on child development are finally acknowledging the extraordinary plasticity and potential of a newborn's brain: in the first six months of life, any healthy baby born into any culture, can learn any language known to humankind. Babies also have an extraordinary capacity for thinking with their full brains; it is later that they learn to think and act linearly, focusing on one task or thought at a time. I believe this is one of the secrets to stepping off the track of linear time and embodying the sacred cyclical in our lives: keep your youthful mind and your childlike innocence!

I remember the very first moment I became consciously aware of myself (it wasn't very glamorous as I had apparently gone in my pajamas and my parents had to change me). Ever since that burst of conscious awareness somewhere between the ages of 1 and 2, I've spent vast volumes of time thinking about how time, consciousness, and evolution relate to one another. Does consciousness require the awareness—and ability to retain—time? If we weren't aware of ourselves, would we still have the concept of time? How does our sense of time affect our development and evolution? Is our passage through and experience of time directly related to consciousness, and what does that really mean?

Now that I have the luxury of a relatively long personal history to reflect upon, I can see cycles within cycles, repeating themes, lessons, patterns. This is my personal cyclical, sacred time, which I must honor if I am to complete my lifepath. Think about yours. Do you see cycles, patterns, or themes? If you don't, look a little deeper. They're uniquely different from mine and from everyone else's, but they're there.

In truth, each phase of life, each journey around the sun that we complete, has something to teach us, something wondrous and magical for us to keep. Fundamental facts of life like birth and death are completely redefined in the context of cyclical, sacred time. Instead of a single, finite line running mercilessly from birth to death, ending in expiration of all of our efforts, experiences, memories, and knowledge, our existence takes on much deeper meaning as vibrant participants in the timeless dance of humanity.

It does take an active, everpresent, conscious awareness of which aspects of our lives we can bring over into sacred time, and which ones we should keep (more or less) linear. And that is a deeply personal choice, for we all live different lives and lead different lifestyles. Each one of us should create and experience our own metamorphosis in our relationship with time—and that is the beauty and the incredible opportunity the Tzolk'in presents us.

We can all become butterflies.

How to Use This Book

The purpose of *The Serpent and the Jaguar* is three-fold: to celebrate the essence of the Tzolk'in through poetic expression, as the Maya themselves do; to help you integrate the energies of this sacred calendar into your daily life; and to enrich your relationship with cyclical time. To that end, the structure of the book is simple:

- "An Introduction to Sacred Time" discusses linear vs. cyclical time;
- The "Mayan Calendar" section provides an overview of the calendar and how it works;
- The "Numbers" section presents the descriptions of the 13 numbers; and
- The main body of the book presents the day signs, the trecenas and all 260 "Energies of the Day."

Trecenas are the 13-day sub-cycles, or Mayan weeks as they are sometimes referred to, that comprise the Tzolk'in. Each trecena begins with a description of its ruling day sign and follows with a discussion of the meaning of that day sign's energy within the context of contemporary society. We then present the daily energies for each of the 13 days of that trecena, then go on to the next trecena, and so on for the full cycle of the calendar.

You can begin following the energies at any point in the Tzolk'in. Regardless of the day you first open this book, you can begin on that day. The Tzolk'in is a cyclical calendar, and therefore has no beginning and no end. Contrary to a great deal of material that has been published, and continues to be written, there is in fact no end to this Mayan Calendar. It did not end on October 28, 2011, it will not end on December 21, 2012, and it will continue to serve humanity as long as there is a human race to appreciate it.

Before you begin, however, it is important to take note of a few essential concepts:

First, each day of the Tzolk'in has its own unique flavor, intention, and meaning. The day signs, which the Maya consider to be masculine in their essence, are complemented by the numbers, considered to be feminine in their essence. Just as in any human relationship involving two individuals, the pairing produces a distinct energy and essence that differs from the energy and essence of the two entities individually. This is not a far-flung comparison; the Maya in fact consider the day signs as sacred entities, whom they call "naguales," influencing the energy of the day they rule. This means there are 260 individual and unique energies, not 20 that repeat every 13 days, as other Mayan astrology resources imply.

To my knowledge, this is the first time the entire cycle of 260 unique daily energies has been presented in published form (apart from the award-winning **MCP Mayan Tzolk'in** mobile app we launched in June 2011, despite my having begun this book prior; it's far quicker to develop an app than it is to write a book!).

Secondly, most books about Mayan astrology focus on describing and explaining the individual day signs and numbers, which is indeed a critical part of the Tzolk'in journey—and especially so if you are interpreting your Mayan birth chart. When it comes to living with the Tzolk'in on a daily basis, however, it takes a different approach. The energies of the Tzolk'in are meant to be interpreted on a daily basis and in the specific personal context of the life and environment of the person working with it. So whether you are living with the Maya, having a Maya Daykeeper read the energies for you every day, or working with the calendar on your own, you should take your personal circumstances carefully into consideration as you read this book and apply the daily energies to your life.

The Energies of the Day are meant to serve you as a guide, a path, a horizon to orient your life toward, not a formula or an absolute to follow to the letter. You are a key partner in this relationship with the Tzolk'in—it is, after all, *your* relationship. Much like in the philosophy of Eastern medicine that holds the patient responsible for his or her health, you are responsible for your destiny and your relationship with time.

Finally, there is the all-important question of *When do the energies begin?* You, the readers of this book, live in many different regions of the globe and orient your schedules to many different time zones. How can the energies of a given day possibly apply in Europe at the same time as in Latin America, for the same day? The answer is, they don't. While this particular question remains a point of some controversy among the Maya themselves, with some Daykeepers arguing that there is in fact a temporal "ground zero" for each day—and that ground zero is of course located in Central America, the Maya motherland—many of the older Daykeepers will tell you two things:

- That the energies of a given day begin flowing around midnight or sunrise;
- That it is perfectly acceptable to use your own local time zone as your temporal "ground zero."

Resist the temptation to think that at the stroke of midnight, whereever you are in the world, the previous day's energy passes the baton to the next, and in a split second it's suddenly the new energy reigning over the land. Remember that the Maya relate to time in a cyclical, organic manner, not the rigid, linear way we in the "industrialized world" do. There are no deadlines. Things simply flow. Much like you cannot easily mark where one wave ends in the ocean and the next one starts, it is equally challenging to try and pinpoint the exact moment between the energies of two subsequent days, because there simply is no such precise moment. Let's say the day 7 Ik' is winding down. You may feel the wind slow to a breeze, and start sensing the arrival of 8 Akb'al. In fact, you may become aware of a transition, an overlap of the two, for a certain period of time as the day itself ebbs into night and then into sunrise of the next day. Ik's final breezes mellow out into the soft quiet night of Akb'al's potential.

And so, if you imagine the sun's rays slipping over the curvature of the Earth, embracing each sliver of longitude as the planet spins around its axis, so too do the Tzolk'in's energies wash over our world, waves in an endless ocean of time, as each one of us awakens to a brand new day.

Let's get started

Ready to dive in? If you're completely new to the Mayan Calendar and this is one of the first books you're reading about the Tzolk'in calendar, it is strongly recommended you read the *Introduction* and the two sections on the Tzolk'in and the numbers before you turn to the main body of the book: *The Day Signs, the Trecenas and the Energies of the Day.*

If you've been studying the Tzolk'in for some time and are familiar with how the calendar works and the meanings of the numbers, I still recommend reading the *Introduction* before the main body, as a reminder of the importance of cyclical time.

You may also wish to read through the *Explanatory Notes* as additional points of interest.

As someone who lives with the calendar on a daily basis, I will share my own personal recommendations with you. They are, however, just that: recommendations, suggestions. Things that have worked for me, and also many others. But there is no template, no formula, no "rules" to how to enter or experience any of the days of the sacred Tzolk'in. No roadmap, no directions, no Google Maps. We each hold within us the guideline, the path that is most natural for our growth and evolution; but we do need to be patient and quiet our minds so that we may hear the songs our higher souls are singing to us.

A brief key to reading the Energies of the Day

The main section of the book, *The Day Signs, The Trecenas, and the Energies of the Day* is where you will most likely spend most of your time. This section lists the 260 Energies of the Day of the Tzolk'in, organized by trecenas. Each trecena, or set of 13 days, begins with the ruling day sign for that trecena and follows with the individual Energies of the Day.

As clarified in the *Explanatory Notes*, we begin the line-up with Caban, which is considered by the K'iche' Maya as the first day sign. However, don't feel obliged to wait until the next iteration of 1 Caban to start living with the energies. Books—at least those in print—are linear works, so we've got to "start" somewhere, but the

Tzolk'in is a cyclical calendar, so you can jump in literally anywhere: 9 Akb'al, 13 Ix, or 8 Kan. All you need is to know what Tzolk'in day it is on any given Gregorian date. For example, if you want to read the Energy of the Day for November 1, 2011, you would turn to 4 Kan in this book.

To calculate the Mayan (Tzolk'in) date, you can do so manually by turning to the "Mayan Calendar Tables" section on page 243 and following the instructions printed there, or go online and use our free Tzolk'in calculator at **http://www.maya-portal.net/tzolkin**, or any other online calculator that uses the K'iche' day count, which is widely considered to be the most accurate (be sure you're using an authentic Tzolk'in calculator, however, as there are a few that claim authenticity but in reality either are Dreamspell calculators or use an erroneous count. You want to make sure you're using the Goodman-Martinez-Thompson (GMT) correlation constant of 584,283).

If you happen to have a printed calendar or agenda with the Tzolk'in days listed for each Gregorian day, that's fine as well, but again be sure the count is accurate. You can always cross-check other sources against our online Tzolk'in calculator.

But once you've got the Mayan date, how, you might ask, do you find 4 Kan in a sea of no fewer than 260 energies? It's quite simple—you just need to know the trecena that 4 Kan falls under, then locate that trecena in the Table of Contents in this book. To do that, you turn to the Calendar Board on page 244 and find Kan on the lefthand side. Run your finger along the Kan row, until you find the number 4 (you'll pass the numbers 8, 2, 9, 3, and 10). Then, move up the column to find the number 1, which is the beginning of the 13 days of which 4 Kan is a part, and run your finger back to the left along that row. You'll hit the day sign Imix. And that, indeed, is the trecena where you will find 4 Kan. The Imix trecena starts on page 123; and on page 127, you will find... 4 Kan.

You will see that each Energy of the Day has the full name of the Tzolk'in day on one side of the page, first in Yucatec and directly below in K'iche'. Directly opposite are the glyphs, or graphical representations, of the number and the day sign. Below the glyphs and the printed name of the Tzolk'in day is the Energy of the Day.

Here is an example:

Uaxac (8) Chuen
Wajxaqib' (8) B'atz'

For the K'iche' Maya, Wajxaqib' B'atz' (Uaxac Chuen) is the first day of the sacred Tzolk'in calendar, and marks a period of festivities and celebrations. ... Uaxac and Chuen both embody the weaving of life, the thread of time, and the sacred energy of birth. This makes today a blessed day for such sacred rites as weddings, engagements, anniversaries, baby announcements, and other events marking the union of two people or the birth of a new life.

Uaxac Chuen is "8 Chuen" in Yucatec; *Wajxaqib' B'atz'*, directly below, is the K'iche' version. Since the vast majority of readers are more familiar with the Yucatec terms, I reference the Yucatec in the Energy of the Day texts.

Give the Tzolk'in its time

Above all, give this journey time. If you feel drawn to the Mayan Calendar and wish to enter those realms deeper and more profound within your own soul and destiny, to discover your own personal truth and the path to a fulfilling spiritual life, you've got to give it time. It might be a little ironic that you need time to understand a calendar, but the Tzolk'in isn't just a series of numbers and names of days and months. It's a way of relating to and living in sacred time that has been explored, practiced, and refined by the people of Mesoamerica for thousands of years—and still is today.

You may resonate with the energies of the Tzolk'in right away, or not at all for several weeks or months. Whatever your particular experience, do not take it for granted and do not give up. The idea isn't to "conquer" the Tzolk'in, use it for a while, and then go on with your life. If you want the full experience, the full benefits of this sacred calendar, you have to let it become a part of your consciousness just as the Western, the Gregorian calendar is ingrained into your life. Try not to skip a day if you can; even if you just read the Energy of the Day once and don't think about it again, it will play in the background of your consciousness as you get on with your day.

Just as importantly, take the time to get to know each number and day sign. Treat each day as if it were a newborn child, because, in truth, it is. Each and every day that dawns upon our planet is a blessing, a rare and sacred pearl in the vast cosmos surrounding us. Perhaps this is why there is something so magical about the dawn—like newborn babies, the day is at its purest, freshest, most innocent. Perhaps that is why so many people rise just before dawn to meditate, to reconnect with that innocence and purity.

Listen to your inner silence

The ideal way to align your life with the Tzolk'in is to read the energy for each coming day the night before, ideally in a quiet place. This can be a room in your house, your garden, a nearby park, the beach at dusk, or anywhere you feel most tranquil. Reflect or meditate upon the incoming energy and its relation to your life, and give thanks to the outgoing energy of the day that is now ending. Take in what you've learned from the outgoing energy and look forward to the imminent illuminations of the incoming.

It is equally valuable to spend time with the incoming energy. If you have time in the early morning, or are willing to rise a few minutes earlier than usual, spend a few moments welcoming the fresh new energy of the day that's just dawning before you, opening your consciousness and your life to the guidance it can give you. Reflect upon what the new energy means to you, how you can use it today, or what you can learn from it.

It is important that you are not disturbed or interrupted during either of these meditations. If your attention is requested unexpectedly, and you are obliged to respond, accept the interruption as an innocent act of the external world and resume your meditation when you are alone again.

These "meditations" do not have to be performed in the classic meditation pose, your legs crossed, back straight, eyes closed, your hands resting on your knees, turned up with the thumb and forefinger forming an O—although that is a wonderful way to quiet the mind and align your vital energies. Employ whatever position and orientation works for you so that you are not interrupted either by external events or your own restless thoughts.

Your meditations also do not have to be long. Do not think that if you don't spend a full 30 minutes meditating on the energies each day, you're somehow being lazy or selling the Tzolk'in short. We all have busy lives, and sometimes having a half hour to ourselves in peace is simply not possible. Instead, try spending several brief moments in inner silence, throughout the day—wherever you happen to be: sitting in your car at a traffic light, standing in line at the grocery store, waiting for a client to show up at a meeting. You'll be amazed how quickly these previously maddening tests of patience turn into mini time spas you can never get enough of. Not to mention how much more stress-free you'll feel.

Align your consciousness with sacred time

For those of us used to living with the no-nonsense, business-like Gregorian calendar, it can be a bit of a stretch to integrate not only a completely different timekeeping system (260 instead of 365 days, 13-day weeks, and no specific beginning or end), but also a vastly different *conception* of time—the concept of sacred time discussed in the *Introduction*.

The ancient Maya lived—and their descendants continue to do so today—with both ordinary and sacred concepts of time. They use their solar Haab calendar, which is closer to our Gregorian, for agriculture, accounting, and other practical matters, while the Tzolk'in serves a deeply personal and spiritual purpose.

Each Energy of the Day in this book is an interpretation of the *combined* energies of the day sign and the number, taken within the underlying context of the current trecena as well as the society we live in. This is the key to the daily energies of the Tzolk'in. The energy produced by the union of the day sign and the number takes on a different flavor and essence than that of the day sign and the number individually. In other words, each day's energy is unique. We could in fact go so far as to say that every single day that has ever dawned on Earth, has been like no other before or after. That sure takes the boredom out of life, doesn't it!

As you read each Energy of the Day, let the words soak in at first, with no filters and no judgment. You might in fact spend one entire cycle of the Tzolk'in getting to know the day signs, the numbers, and their combined energies. Whenever you are ready, start to adapt the daily energies to your life, your personal circumstances, and to the environment in which you live, work, and play. Remember that you do not need to take the daily energies at their face value, as a strict recipe to be followed to the letter. If an Energy of the Day feels exactly right, go with it. If it feels right in terms of context but not specifics or details, reflect on how your particular situation applies to the energies of that day and whether there might be a different angle to or perspective on the Energy of the Day that works better for you. And if you're not resonating with a daily energy at all, re-read the descriptions of the day sign and the number and reflect on how that blend of energies could work for you. Try to create your own interpretation.

Note also any cyclical patterns in your life in general—over larger spans of time than just day to day. The Maya consider that a person becomes an Elder at 52 years of age, a length of time they divide into four periods of 13 years each (note the reference to the sacred number 13). Even as the Tzolk'in cycles through twenty phases of 13 days on a rolling basis, so we pass through four periods of 13 years before we finally achieve elderhood.

Each one of us is unique. Each one of us sees the world we live in in a different light—and each one of us is likely to interpret the 260 daily energies printed in this book, a bit differently. And that's precisely the purpose of the Tzolk'in—to support and enlighten us as we explore our personal relationship with sacred time.

Some Maya Daykeepers say that all of the energies of the Tzolk'in are ever present, every day. For them the calendar is a vast energetic ocean whose currents run deep below the surface; each individual day brings forth the waves and peaks of certain energies that rise to rule that day. As the day unfolds, its composite energy, created by the confluence of a day sign and a number, blooms into myriad possible expressions. It is this deep ocean of possibility and potential we swim in every day of our lives, but too often without realizing it. The Tzolk'in is the ship to help us navigate these profound waters.

Allow the sacred days of the Tzolk'in to become your friends, your guides, not your enemy or the source of your stress. If you find yourself feeling frustration, anger, guilt, or other negative emotions as you seek to integrate this calendar into your life, notice and recognize them, but let them go. Sentiments like that are toxic, and there is always another day to look forward to. If you don't get everything done that you wanted to on a given day, release your ambitions—fretting about productivity benchmarks, to-do lists, and deadlines is a linear mindset. Remember the Tzolk'in is cyclical. You may go many days without any apparent illumination or alignment. Perhaps sooner than you think, there may come a day where things just fall into place—and that will have been the culmination of diverse energies building up to that moment.

Honor the Tzolk'in

Living with the Tzolk'in is not about laws of attraction. If you're looking for increasing your wealth, finding your soulmate, or building a dream career, the Tzolk'in won't help you do it any faster than any other astrological system in the world. That is not its purpose; and anyone who promises that is not being sincere. You may indeed attain your greatest dreams while living with the Tzolk'in, and that would not be unheard of. But the purpose of this calendar is far greater: to support and uplift human spiritual evolution through the merged worldviews of cyclical and linear time.

For the Maya, a day is more than just the passage of the sun, a certain period of time marked by the revolution of the Earth around its axis. It is a sacred event, an awe-inspiring phenomenon that has repeated, without fail, ever since our planet was born. In turn, the day signs of the Tzolk'in are entities or naguales, "spirit guides" that influence, support, and protect the days, and as such should be honored and respected.

We take the day, and the many other astronomical and planetary phenomena that make human life possible, for granted. We take time itself, and often our share of it, for granted. It's time to renew the awe and wonder we felt when we were children, when we had magic in our lives. It's time to start living in sacred time.

THE MAYAN CALENDAR

That which we call the Mayan Calendar might more accurately be termed "the Mesoamerican Calendar," for it was common to almost all the peoples of ancient Mexico. It was so profoundly intertwined into the fabric of the cultures of this region that it survives to this day, despite repeated, brutal attempts at complete eradication—along with the descendants of the Maya, the people who brought this calendar to modern-day consciousness. In fact, one could say that the use of the Mesoamerican Calendar, along with pyramid temples, shared mythologies, and a reverence for jade, defines the entire region as a civilization. The calendar may well be as old as Mesoamerican civilization itself. Many scholars have credited the invention of this calendar—often called the Sacred Calendar because of its powerful spiritual significance—to the Olmecs, the oldest of the Mesoamerican cultures, which is thought to have begun at about 1,200 BC. The most recent research, however, suggests that the calendar we know today as the Mayan Calendar may have originated in small villages of hunter-gatherers as early as 3,000 BC.

At its most basic and fundamental level, this Mayan, or Mesoamerican, Calendar features two timekeeping systems: the Tzolk'in or "ritual almanac" of 260 days, comprised of twenty symbolic day signs and thirteen numbers (13 x 20 = 260), cycling endlessly with no dependence on astronomical phenomena, and the Haab', a solar calendar of 365 days (eighteen 20-day months called *winals*, followed by a rest period of 5 days called the *wayeb*).

Although they are standalone calendars in their own right, the Tzolk'in and the Haab' interlock with one another like cogs in a wheel. Because 260 and 365 have a common factor of 5, the shortest amount of time it takes for the same two Tzolk'in and Haab' positions to re-occur (for example, 13 Akb'al 10 Yaxkin, which are Tzolk'in and Haab' dates, respectively) is once every 52 years (260 x 365) / 5 = 18980 days, or 52 x 365 days). This 52-year cycle is called a "Calendar Round."

These two calendar systems were common to almost all peoples of ancient Mesoamerica. They are still in use today among traditional peoples, especially the Tzolk'in. The ancient solar calendar Haab is much more rare, but the Ki'che' Maya of highland Guatemala still use both. This book focuses exclusively on the Tzolk'in, the personal astrological calendar the Maya used for their intimate daily lives, for guiding the destiny of their lifepaths, for determining personal compatibility for love, business, or friendship, and for raising their children in respectful resonance of their own day signs, not the expectations or unfulfilled dreams of the parents.

The Meaning of the Day Signs and Numbers

The K'iche' Maya of highland Guatemala refer to the core of the Tzolk'in as the "Sacred Counter of Days and Time." The day signs and the numbers of the Tzolk'in each have their own spirit, or essence; in addition, the day signs are often referred to as "naguales," or spirit guides that rule certain elements or aspects of life. This is because the day signs are considered to be the primary archetypes of human character—in fact, they embody the essential myths and archetypes of the ancient lands of the Maya. The day signs carry a masculine energy, while the numbers are considered feminine in nature; but these concepts do not carry the same meanings that they do in "industrialized" societies. (For a more detailed discussion on this, please see "The Numbers" section immediately following.)

Each of the Tzolk'in's twenty day signs holds the sacred role of shaping and influencing the character and destiny of a person, which is based on the combined energies of their Mayan birth sign and number. For the Maya, each person brings with them their innate character, abilities, professional preference, and other traits already at birth. This is why it is so important to respect our children and allow them to grow into the people they were born to be, rather than to impose our own desires and dreams upon them. This of course applies to us, as well—easy to say, much more difficult to achieve, but it is the first step to true self-realization. The Maya understand this innately; for many of us, it takes a bit of reminding since our lives overflow with a deluge of media messages telling us who the marketers want us to be.

In the two tables that follow, you can see the names of the twenty day signs and the thirteen numbers, in both Yucatec and K'iche' Maya.

Table 1.
THE NAMES OF THE DAY SIGNS

YUCATEC	K'ICHE'
Caban	No'j
Etznab	Tijax
Cauac	Kawoq
Ahau	Ajpu
Imix	Imox
Ik'	Iq'
Akb'al	Aq'ab'al
Kan	K'at
Chicchan	Kan
Cimi	Kame
Manik'	Kej
Lamat	Q'anil
Muluc	Toj
Oc	Tz'i
Chuen	B'atz'
Eb	E
Ben	Aj
Ix'	I'x
Men	Tz'ikin
Cib	Ajmaq

While many of you will be familiar with, and perhaps expecting, Imix as the "first" day sign, it should be made clear that Imix is not, in fact, the first day sign of the Tzolk'in. As is discussed at various places in the book, the Tzolk'in is a cyclical, endless calendar, and as such has no actual start or end point. Of course, this being a book with linearly laid-out pagination, we do need to start somewhere with these lists, so I have chosen Caban, out of respect for the practice of the K'iche' Maya, who consider Caban to be the initial day sign (when it comes to listing the signs). The "Explanatory Notes" section at the end of the book goes into greater detail on this topic.

Table 2.
THE NAMES OF THE NUMBERS

NUMERAL	YUCATEC	K'ICHE'
1	Hun	Jun
2	Ka	Kieb
3	Ox	Oxib'
4	Kan	Kahib'
5	Ho	Job'
6	Uac	Wakib'
7	Uuc	Wukub'
8	Uaxac	Wajxaqib'
9	Bolon	B'elejeb'
10	Lahun	Lajuj
11	Buluk	Junlajuj
12	La Ka	Kablajuj
13	Oxlahun	Oxlajuj

The Long Count Calendar

The so-called "end date" of December 21, 2012, that so many Westerners ask about, is based on the linear time-keeping system known as the Long Count, which was used to compute large cosmic and historical cycles. The Long Count endowed the Maya with a sense of cosmic vision that made them unique. Though all Mesoamerican civilizations made use of the Sacred Calendar, only the Classic Period Maya practiced the Long Count. Whether or not they were the ones who invented it, they certainly adapted it as their own and made it one of the foundation stones of their culture. In a way, it is a measure of their unique mathematical and philosophical gifts. The Great Cycle—that span of time which began in 3114 BC and ends upon the much heralded event of December 21, 2012—is part of the Long Count. With the invention of the Great Cycle, the Maya were making a bold and powerful effort to mathematically quantify and define the cycles of world emergence. The Mayan mathematical system is a vigesimal system, meaning it's based on orders of twenty—as in, one, twenty, four hundred, eight thousand, and so on—rather our own decimal system, which is based on orders of ten—as in, one, ten, hundred, thousand, and so on.

Although the Maya and other Mesoamerican societies had the Haab, a solar year of 365 days, the Long Count is based upon a "mathematical year" of 360 k'in (days), called a tun, which means "stone" in Mayan. Twenty tuns (7,200 days) was a k'atun, which means "twenty stones." Twenty k'atuns (400 tuns or 144,000 days), constituted a b'ak'tun, meaning "a bundle of stones." Thirteen b'ak'tuns made up a Great Cycle, which adds up to 5,200 tuns and 260 k'atuns. All Long Count dates contain the following elements, written in this order: the b'ak'tun, the k'atun, the tun, the winal or 20-day period, and the k'in or day. A Mayan date such as 9.12.2.0.16 (July 5, 674 AD) means that 9 b'ak'tuns, 12 k'atuns, 2 tuns, 0 winals, and 16 k'ins have passed since the creation date in 3114 BC.

Those who perceive the end of the Great Cycle as a catastrophe or cataclysm may wish to note that the Maya conceived of epochs or ages that were much longer than the Great Cycle. A p'iktun was comprised of 8,000 tuns or 20 b'ak'tuns. A kalabtun was 160,000 tuns, and a kinchiltun was 3,200,000 tuns. The present p'iktun will end on October 13, 4772 AD, a date that was carved in the Temple of the Inscriptions at Palenque.

The Tzolk'in and Mesoamerican Mythology

The Tzolk'in forms the basis of much Mayan magic and ritual; it is a system of astrology as well as divination. People such as the Maya, the Toltecs, the Aztecs, and the Hopi all shared a concept which we might call "cycles of emergence." According to this shared cultural view, the world has been created and destroyed a number of times. Each world the gods brought into being was created with the hope that humankind would worship the divine powers properly; more often than not, of course, the gods were disappointed. Their continuing attempts to create a perfect being, one who will honor the sacred, is the foundation of evolution.

The Hopi say that humankind has been successively "emerging" through four different worlds. The world is always in a state of emergence, never static. It is constantly developing, and hence unstable; it must therefore be maintained. It is only through the prayers of human beings and their spiritual behavior that the world can be brought into equilibrium.

The idea of humankind's spiritual evolution lies at the heart of the history of the cosmos as the Maya understood it. Because each world carries with it the same eternal, recurring process, their view of the universe is circular, like that of other indigenous traditions. But the concept of continuing evolution also gives the Mesoamerican world view a linear quality, a sense of ongoing development. In Mayan thought, the linear and the circular world views are combined into what we might describe as a spiral, inherently circular but forever upward-moving.

As you can see, the Mayan Calendar system is a universe of cycles within cycles, each with its own essence, myth, and meaning, yet all of them interrelated, intertwined, just as the orbits of the planets interlock within the solar system, and the solar system in turn forms part of a complex network of stars within the galaxy. Embodying sacred geometries, mathematics, astronomy, science, and spirituality, the Mayan Calendar system is perhaps one of the greatest legacies that the ancient Mesoamerican civilization has created for the rest of the human race.

It is this uplifting, forward-looking worldview that we have tried to instill into every aspect of the Mayan Calendar Portal and the projects produced beneath its umbrella, including this book, for the benefit of all. Thank you for sharing this journey with us.

THE NUMBERS

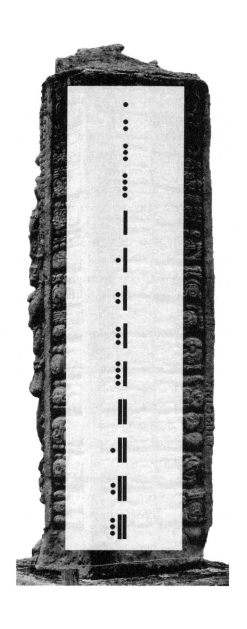

THE NUMBERS

In the Mesoamerican worldview, which includes astrology, it is customary to regard the nature of all things in terms of cosmic polarities. This concept has many names: yin and yang, masculine and feminine, light and dark. In the Judeo-Christian tradition, the tendency is to assign moral values to polarities: light is good, or positive, while dark is bad, or negative; the masculine tends to be "tough" or "strong" while the feminine tends to be "soft" or "weak." In Mesoamerican astrology, there are no such values. Instead, each polarity embodies its own unique blend of energies, reflecting the complexity of life. In the Tzolk'in, some day signs may indeed have primarily positive characteristics, while others may be more volatile. But there are no absolutes. There is no such thing as an "evil day sign" or an "angelic number."

For the purposes of reference only, we will employ the terms "masculine" and "feminine" to describe the polarities of the Tzolk'in. The 13 numbers of the Tzolk'in are considered essentially feminine in nature, while the 20 day signs are primarily masculine—yet each day sign and number have some measure of both. Like most things in life, it's never quite black and white.

According to author Ken Johnson, who has spent many years studying and living the sacred calendar with the K'iche' Maya of Guatemala, the Maya regard the numbers as spiritual companions of the day signs. The pairing of a number and a day sign is, in essence, a sacred marriage of energies and influences, an alchemical union of dual polarities. While the day signs are naguales, or spirit guides, the numbers are external and represent personality factors, rather than archetypes. They are the spices that flavor the dish.

The K'iche' Daykeepers of Guatemala say that the low numbers embody weaker or softer traits, the high numbers are so strong and intense they could be potentially dangerous, and the middle numbers are the most balanced. In some ways, that is far too simplistic an illustration. Each number has unique, individual characteristics, its own positive as well as challenging aspects. We can say, however, that in general, even numbers manifest their positive qualities with greater facility, while odd numbers are regarded as more intense and take a bit more work to express their "good" side. Yet there are exceptions even to this general rule: the number 9 is an odd number but is considered a powerful, extremely positive number, so much so that it is used for sacred and ritual purposes.

There is symbolism not just within the numbers but in the fact that there are 13 numbers in the Tzolk'in. The number 13 refers to the 13 heavens of the ancient Mayan Otherworld and the 13 lunar months in the year (approximately 28 days each). It also represents humanity on a physical level—there are 13 joints in the human body: the neck, shoulders, elbows, wrists, hips, knees, and ankles. In his book "Mayan Calendar Astrology," Ken Johnson reveals a little-known link between the feminine, the masculine, and the soul as it relates to numbers in Mayan cosmology. For the Maya, the conscious soul that leaves the body at death is yin (feminine), while the eternal soul, which corresponds to our birth sign and can detach from the physical body, is yang (masculine). This also means that the 13 joints of the human body are related to the feminine, bodily part of the soul, yet it is precisely in these 13 joints that the sacred *koyopa* energy, the Maya version of kundalini, vibrates, much like the chakras of the Hindu philosophy. Maya shamans connect to the *koyopa* to seek profound spiritual or visionary insights, so in essence, in Ken's words, "the *koyopa* which makes shamanic vision possible is itself feminine!"

The ancient Maya associated each of the 13 numbers with a patron deity, or god. For reasons of brevity, we shall not go into depth on this aspect of the numbers in this book. For more information on this topic, consult the Resources section in the back.

As you contemplate the essence and meaning of the numbers throughout the next 13 pages, I'd like to leave you with a provocative thought that Ken Johnson put forth during one of our conversations: 9 is not only the number associated with women and with the feminine, it is also associated with the ancestors. If women and ancestors share the same number in the Tzolk'in, does this suggest that the Maya were once matriarchal?

HUN / JUN
The Number One   ●

Hun, or Jun in K'iche' Maya, is the number One in the sacred Tzolk'in calendar. It represents the beginning of all things, all that is first and all that initiates.

The number One symbolizes the original energy of creation, the power of thought, of inspiration, of the conception and seeding of all things. It represents unity, stability, strength, solidity, resolve of will, and resoluteness of character.

The deity associated with the number One is the Young Moon Goddess, an avatar of the Maize God and the patron of queens.

One may be both a low and an odd number, which are normally considered weak and difficult, but it is nothing of the kind. It holds tremendous power. This is the initiating energy behind all things that inspires us to imagine, to conceive, and to create; to bring ideas and concepts into being. This is the number that ushers in each new trecena and its incoming energies.

Maya Daykeepers typically conduct rituals for all manner of things on a One day; in fact, some traditional Mayan communities dedicate special shrines to this number.

Persons born on a One day will remain firm, confident, and filled with strength and resolution in any situation or circumstance. They will give a strong push to initiate projects or put things into motion, but they tend not to be attentive to details or see things through to the end. For this reason they often need the collaboration of others to help bring ideas to full fruition.

KA / KIEB
The Number Two

K a, or Kieb in K'iche' Maya, is the number Two in the sacred Tzolk'in calendar. It is the symbol of the dual nature of things, of the dichotomy of all things in existence, of opposing yet complementary elements.

The deity associated with the number Two is a bit of a mystery. It seems to embody Duality; and the Maya scholar J. Eric Thompson called him the God of Sacrifices.

The number Two represents duality, polarity, the positive and the negative. It symbolizes all dual states or faces of any concept or aspect of life: birth and death, tranquility and suffering, joy and sadness, night and day, darkness and light, male and female, good and bad, right and wrong, and so on. Life is a struggle: it has its positive and its negative side. There are good days and bad days. Blue sky follows thunder and lightning. Like waves in the ocean, things can go up and down.

Like the Taoists, the Maya perceive the world in terms of cosmic polarities. This concept is embedded in their mythology—here, the number Two figures quite heavily: there are two Hero Twins, two key Lords of the Underworld, and the two monkey twins who represent the day sign Chuen (B'atz'). And there is the eternal dichotomy inherent in all things and all aspects of life: birth and death, light and dark, hot and cold, up and down, the present world and the Underworld, and so on. This theme weaves a common line in all of Mayan myth, especially in the sacred book the *Popol Vuh*.

A person born on a Two day can have twice the strength, will, and power of people born on any other day. Yet Two people can also be indecisive, for the same reason—they can draw upon either side of the cosmic polarities or stand right in the middle, undecided.

OX / OXIB'
The Number Three   ● ● ●

Ox, or Oxib' in K'iche' Maya, is the number Three in the sacred Tzolk'in calendar. It represents doubt, risk, obstruction, insecurity and uncertainty.

In Maya culture, the number Three symbolizes the three cosmic hearth stones that the gods laid down at the beginning of Creation. These stones, also reflected in the belt of Orion, are the foundation of all family and domestic life.

The deity associated with the number Three is the Wind God, the Lord of Breath, which is an aspect of the famed K'uk'ulkan.

Both a low and an odd numeral, Three is the most difficult number in the Tzolk'in. A Three day can bring in energies that ruin preparations or push plans off track, prevent the realization or completion of projects and activities, and cause things not to work out as intended. In fact, many traditional Daykeepers avoid initiating new projects altogether on a Three day. Better to wait for a day or a more appropriate time.

Three is also one of the most challenging birth numbers. Persons born on a Three day tend to be uncertain, indecisive, and overly influenced by external factors and pressures—unless they remain close to home, close to their source. They do better in familiar environments or circumstances than out there in the world at large. They can also typically find their real strength in other areas of the Tzolk'in pantheon of day signs and numbers.

KAN / KAHIB'
•••• The Number Four

K an, or Kahib' in K'iche' Maya, is the number Four in the sacred Tzolk'in calendar. It symbolizes wholeness, completeness, stability, and the sacred geometries inherent in natural and astronomical cycles: there are four cardinal directions, four elements (fire, water, earth and air) four seasons in the year, four key points of the sun's proximity to the Earth (the solstice and the equinox), and four phases of the day (morning, afternoon, evening and night). Four is also the number of dimensions in which we experience most of our conscious life.

The deity associated with the number Four is Ahau, the Sun God as cosmic lord and the god of kings. The word *ahau* means "lord," and the word for "day" (*k'in* in Yucatec or *q'ij* in K'iche') is the same as the word for "sun." This is why Kan, Four, is a solar number—a day is one complete passage of the sun. In fact, the symbol for the number four is often found in Maya hieroglyphs from the Classic period, including the *k'in* hieroglyph.

In Mayan mythology, four pillars hold up the Earth and Sky and four roads lead to Xibalba, the ancient Mayan Underworld. Four also represents the four colors of corn: red, yellow, black and white, which correspond to the four cardinal directions of the East, South, West and North, and the four races of humanity: Native American, Indo-European, African and Asian. There is evidence that the Classic Maya divided the universe into four sections marked by the two intersections of the Milky Way with the ecliptic. To this day, the Maya lay out their ritual altars in a four-point pattern.

Persons born on a Four day have many powers, and can draw on their internal completeness in order to manifest many strengths, abilities and potentialities. They carry a stable, grounded energy that helps set the guidelines for all manner of relationships and interactions, whether on a personal, societal, economic, political or other levels.

HO / JOB'
The Number Five   ▬▬▬

H o, or Job' in K'iche' Maya, is the number Five in the sacred Tzolk'in calendar. It represents the numbers and symmetries embedded in the human experience.

This refers to the human hand and the human foot, with their five fingers and toes, respectively; the five senses (although a few rare and fortunate people have a sixth sense); and the five stages of life—childhood, youth, adulthood, mature adult, elder.

The deity associated with the number Five is the God of Order and Time.

A person born on a Five day is an early bird. She or he is the first to achieve, to reach a goal, and in fact may be ahead of her or his time. At times, however, their tendency to rush into things without planning or forethought may lead "Five" people into awkward or potentially harmful situations.

Uac, or Wakib' in K'iche' Maya, is the number Six in the sacred Tzolk'in calendar. It symbolizes ultimate stability in all aspects of life, but in particular the stability and vitality of the family.

According to the Maya perspective, the stability of the family is based on six facets: 1.) health; 2.) understanding; 3.) work/employment; 4.) friendship; 5.) property or possessions; 6.) positive and negative actions. Each one of these six foundations affects the other as they are all closely interrelated. If the family lacks any of the six, it suffers. For example, if a family lacks employment, the finances as well as the self-esteem of the head of the household will plummet. If there is no understanding and friendship, there will be fights between family members and/or with the neighbors.

In Mayan mythology, the World Tree itself is called "6 Raised-Up Sky," and in modern-day Momostenango, Guatemala, it is the "Place of Number 6," the hill called Paclom, which represents the *axis mundi* or world center. The deity associated with the number Six is an aspect of Chac, the Lightning God.

People born on Six days are very realistic and practical, preferring pragmatic solutions to the challenges in life. Their thoughts and actions are founded in concrete reality rather than wishful or magical thinking.

UUC / WUKUB'
The Number Seven

Uuc, or Wukub' in K'iche' Maya, is the number Seven in the sacred Tzolk'in calendar. It symbolizes unity and neutrality. It also signifies death, closure, and endings.

Sitting at the exact midpoint of the 13 numbers of the Tzolk'in, the number Seven represents the very center of human law and the laws of life: life has its ups and downs, its challenges and its pleasures. It presents us with problems, hardships and failures, but also gives us solutions, opportunities and success. From the vantage point of Seven, all is possible and all is real. The deity associated with the number Seven is one of several Jaguar Gods.

Seven teaches us how a Tzolk'in number can carry one meaning in its basic symbolism and another for personal astrology. For example, to be born on a Seven day is not negative or undesirable; it does not mean death. To be born on a Seven day gives a person the ability to consider all points of view, which can illuminate broad stretches of possibility that others may not see, or render him or her indecisive, unsure which way to go or what decision to take.

In addition, persons born on a Seven day have many opportunities, options and choices that can sway to either extreme: they can choose to create or destroy; to be kind and compassionate or to be tough and heartless; to think in positive and constructive ways or to think negatively and destructively.

But if a Seven native can learn to focus and take decisive action, Seven's power to see things from all angles imparts them with extraordinary creativity and power.

UAXAC / WAJXAQIB'
The Number Eight

Uaxac, or Wajxaqib' in K'iche' Maya, is the number Eight in the sacred Tzolk'in calendar. This is an especially significant number. It embodies the weaving of life, the thread or cord of time, and the sacred energy of birth. It also represents completion and wholeness.

In Maya lore, Eight embodies the concept of the infinity of life and time; the number is often depicted as a ball of thread or as yarn wrapped around the spindle of a spinning wheel. Just as the ball of thread unwinds and unrolls, so do time and life itself unfold. The K'iche' Maya also believe the umbilical cord is composed of eight threads.

The deity associated with the number Eight is the Fertility and Maize God. Mayanist Linda Schele noted that Teosinte, the ancient ancestor of maize, has an ear with exactly eight kernels.

One and Seven represent the beginning and the end, respectively; therefore, since 1 + 7 = 8, Eight symbolizes that union, making it a number of completion or wholeness. This is why the Maya have some kind of ritual for almost every Eight day, and why some deeply traditional communities have a special shrine dedicated to it. In addition, 4 + 4 = 8, so the wholeness of Four doubles with Eight.

Given that Eight is both an even and a middle number, one might expect people born on this day to manifest effortlessly all the highest and most positive qualities of their day sign—and it is true that Eight natives have a great deal of power and ability. Yet as fortunate as they may be, they need to be careful not to overpower others by becoming upset, disturbed or angry. They are also prone to change their minds quickly and easily, and often have mixed feelings about things.

BOLON / B'ELEJEB'
The Number Nine

Bolon, or B'elejeb' in K'iche' Maya, is the number Nine in the sacred Tzolk'in calendar. This is another special number, pregnant with profound symbolism and meaning. An extremely positive number, Nine colors all that it touches with the golden mist of good fortune and propitious energy.

For the Maya, Nine is "the number of life" because it represents the creation and development of human life—there are nine months of human gestation. As a result, Nine is especially associated with women, pregnancy, and the nine lunar cycles of the 260-day Tzolk'in calendar. Curiously, this number is also associated with the ancestors and ancestral wisdom, which begs the question, were the ancient Maya matriarchal societies, or oriented toward the feminine as much as the masculine?

Nine also symbolizes the effort of life as it unfolds, develops and evolves. Life is an unending struggle between often opposing or conflicting forces, situations and experiences, whether it's personal happiness, financial well-being, psychological or physical health and wellness, relationships, professional life and career, and so on.

The ancient Maya of the Classic Period (200 – 900 AD) favored Nine days above all others for the coronations of kings, sacred rituals, and other important ceremonies. In Maya, Toltec, and Aztec mythology, there are nine levels of Xibalba, or the "Nine Hells" as they are called. Some modern-day Maya teachers also refer to the nine steps in the building of a house and nine stages in growing and harvesting crops. The deity associated with the number Nine is the Hero Twin Xbalanque.

A person born on a Nine day is well balanced and can manifest her or his goals and plans without great effort.

LAHUN / LAJUJ
The Number Ten

Lahun, or Lajuj in K'iche' Maya, is the number Ten in the sacred Tzolk'in calendar. It represents human cooperation and collaboration, and symbolizes the bonds and relationships between people. It also represents family, society, and the relationship between a man and a woman. This link to human society comes from Ten's direct correlation to the number of fingers and toes on our hands and feet.

The deity associated with the number Ten is the God of Death. Perhaps this is why the number Ten also symbolizes the ups and downs of life. We enjoy moments of success, advancement and progress, overcoming problems and obstacles, but we also face times of loss, regression and failure. This is neither good nor bad; it is simply how life is, and Ten teaches us to walk that most stable and harmonious of paths—straight down the middle.

A person born on a Ten day is very stable, as we would expect to find among the even numbers. But beneath the surface, Ten natives tend to be quite fragile and extremely vulnerable, and so need to learn how to build up their natural defenses; at the very least to grow a thick skin.

BULUK / JUNLAJUJ
The Number Eleven

Buluk, or Junlajuj in K'iche' Maya, is the number Eleven in the sacred Tzolk'in calendar. This number has tremendous strength, force, and power, which should be used with great care, for like all forces of nature, its power can be extreme and easily overwhelm all efforts to tame or control it. What is more, Eleven is neither positive nor negative; it is completely neutral, symbolizing the sacred balance of life. This is where its danger lies: because it knows no moral value, its power can easily sway violently destructive as it can bloom extraordinarily abundant.

Some Mayan teachers see Eleven as representative of the totality of past, present and future, of everything that develops, evolves or unfolds over time. The deity associated with the number Eleven is an Earth Goddess.

Although it is a high number, which most K'iche' Daykeepers consider as a powerful, intense, and potentially dangerous number, certain Eleven days are considered particularly auspicious: Chicchan, Cimi, Manik', Ben, and Ahau in some communities. Whenever these day signs pair with the number Eleven, local shamans make a pilgrimage to nearby sacred mountains.

A person born on an Eleven day has great potential, but also a tendency to wander through life without direction. He or she needs to remain focused, taking care not to drift aimlessly through life. If they can harness their abilities and focus on their goals, they may prove to be highly creative and successful.

LA KA / KABLAJUJ
The Number Twelve

L a Ka, or Kablajuj in K'iche' Maya, is the number Twelve in the sacred Tzolk'in calendar. This is another particularly powerful and intense number, symbolizing the full substance and essence of life. The deity associated with the number Twelve is the Sky God.

The highest of the even numbers, Twelve represents nothing less than the cumulative sum total of our thoughts and reflections on life, its meaning and its purpose. It embodies the actions we have taken and the goals we've accomplished, the things we have said and the things we have done, the paths we've traveled and the experiences we have had, and all of the family, societal and cultural influences—as well as our own—that have ever come to bear any impact on our lives.

In short, Twelve helps us sum up the full meaning and experience of our lives, at any given point in time. We can certainly use Twelve days to reflect upon the direction of our lives at any moment, and use Twelve's great power to redirect or adjust our current lifepath. This can be extremely useful, in particular at times or in situations where we are feeling hopeless, without direction or guidance.

People born on Twelve days possess an overabundance of energy, power and strength. They are also fiercely independent, and do not need or want others telling them what to do.

OXLAHUN / OXLAJUJ
The Number Thirteen

Oxlahun, or Oxlajuj in K'iche' Maya, is the number Thirteen in the sacred Tzolk'in calendar. Perhaps the most mystical and profound number in the Tzolk'in, Thirteen embodies the ability to develop and harness psychic and spiritual powers, connect and communicate with other worlds and dimensions, forecast future trends, and predict events such as natural disasters and phenomena.

The deity associated with the number Thirteen is the Water Serpent God, associated with entrances to the Underworld, such as pools and the cenotés that can be found throughout the Yucatán.

The number Thirteen represents the thirteen major joints in the human body, and therefore the overall ability for the body to move. The K'iche' Maya of Guatemala believe that *koyopa*, the sacred vital life energy of a human being, courses throughout these joints. The human being and the human body have extraordinary abilities, from physical movement and coordination to creating things of great beauty and utility, but also to develop powerful psychic and spiritual abilities.

For this reason, the K'iche' also consider Thirteen to be a powerful resource for divination readings with the sacred tz'ite seeds—it enhances their accuracy and precision, the ability to feel and perceive signs and signals in the blood (via pulsations), and the related spiritual counseling that typically follows such readings. On Thirteen days, the world of the spirits and ancestors is more easily accessible; these are therefore ideal days to meditate, seek profound insight, and cultivate psychic gifts. Thirteen also represents the completion of all life, all movement and process, and relates to refinement and sensitivity, enhanced perception and acute intuition. All of these abilities apply to all actions performed on a Thirteen day.

A person born on a Thirteen day is likely to have great psychic and spiritual powers—or at least the potential to develop such abilities easily. In fact, she or he may find life difficult or challenging if they fail to do so.

THE DAY SIGNS
THE TRECENAS
AND
THE ENERGIES OF THE DAY

The Day Signs, the Trecenas, and the Energies of the Day

No book about the Tzolk'in calendar can go without descriptions of the numbers and the day signs. The numbers we have just explored; the descriptions of the day signs follow. What is not commonly mentioned in books, web sites, and other sources, are the trecenas—the 20 periods of 13-day "weeks" that make up the 260 days of the Tzolk'in—and still more rarely, if ever at all, the energies of the days themselves. Indeed, this may be the first book in recent history to publish the full set of the energies of the days.

As we know, there are 260 number/day sign combinations, generated as a result of the individual pairing of numbers and day signs. Each day sign is paired with each number only once: there is only one instance of 9 Akb'al, 11 Eb, or 8 Lamat, for example. The energy that results from this union is unique, extremely potent, and embodies much more than the collective sum of the individual meanings of the day sign and the number. Perhaps more importantly, this energy is what I call "stem cell" energy—the very blueprint of potential and possibility, whose manifestation or rendering into reality is intertwined with the individual who integrates that energy into his or her life and consciousness, the circumstances or context in which the energy is used, and the intention with which it is harnessed and employed.

In other words, each one of us will no doubt read any given "Energy of the Day" differently. My interpretation may differ from yours; your loved one, your neighbor, your co-worker may use the energies in completely different ways or contexts, for wildly diverse reasons or intentions. No matter how acutely these individual interpretation diverge, they are all valid and all useful (assuming the proper methodology for or approach to interpreting the energies is being employed). This is the beauty of the Tzolk'in: it is an endlessly rich, profoundly complex yet extraordinarily simple energetic ecosystem that supports and nourishes the full range of human experience.

Like a four-dimensional fractal, the Tzolk'in functions on multiple levels, its energies and structures nestled one into the other like the shell of a Nautilus or the petals of a rose: at the most granular level are the daily energies. String 13 of them together and you've got a trecena. Twenty of those create a full Tzolk'in cycle, and that cycle is itself interwoven with the solar year and with greater cycles of time called *k'atuns*, spanning about 20 years each. As Ken Johnson puts it, "a symphony of cycles within cycles."

The word "trecena" comes from the Spanish word *trece*, which means *thirteen*. Each trecena runs from the number 1 through the number 13, then gives way to the next trecena, the numbers cycle through again, and so on for 20 trecenas until the Tzolk'in cycle completes. Because there are 20 day signs but only 13 numbers, each trecena starts with a different day sign—and again, each day sign can launch a trecena only once. While the numbers give shape and structure to the trecena, it's the day sign that "rules" this period, infusing it with a subtle undercurrent of its energy. For the purposes of easy reference, each trecena starts off with a description of the ruling day sign, followed by an exploration of the meaning of the trecena in the context of contemporary society, and then the 13 individual daily energies.

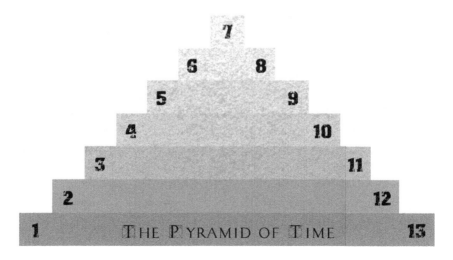

THE PYRAMID OF TIME

As we shared in "The Numbers" section above, the K'iche' Daykeepers of Guatemala consider the low numbers weak, the middle numbers balanced, and the high numbers strong. While this is not the only approach to working with the Tzolk'in, the calendar practices of the K'iche' Maya are considered to be the most closely aligned with those of the ancient Maya (the Classic Period). The K'iche' Daykeepers perform all major rituals mid-trecena, on the days of balanced energy. As Ken Johnson explains, the cycle of the trecena is best shown as a pyramid—the conceptual equivalent of the 13 Heavens that were part of the cosmology of ancient Mexico (see the illustration above).

Ken has a wonderful way of describing the trecena cycles:

"Each trecena cycle may be regarded as a particular quantum of energy, an energy that travels in a wave-like motion. Precisely like a wave, it begins as an underground surge, symbolized by the sun's emergence from the Underworld on the first day of the cycle. This wave of energy grows in power until it crests. Then it begins to descend, discharging its quantum of energy in a thundering crash to the shore. As the energy inherent in the wave trickles away into the sand on the night of the thirteenth day, a new wave cycle has already begun farther out at sea. The power of the day sign that will begin the new trecena is already present. At sunset on the thirteenth day, the Daykeepers welcome the spirit of the coming day, the one who will begin the next trecena cycle. They think of the next day as a 'guest' who is already entering the sacred space."

The next 200 pages will take you on a journey through the energy cycles of the Tzolk'in. All 260 daily energies, all 20 day signs, all 20 trecenas. But unlike most travels, this path neither begins nor ends: you can start on any of the days, any of the trecenas, any of the day signs, at any time. You can stop the journey, then pick it up again at any time. The key is to keep going, regardless of how many days you miss. They will all come back round again.

Whatever day you first dive in, may you have an enjoyable and illuminating journey.

Caban / No'j
Ruler of the Trecena of Introspection

*original artwork, printed here in black & white,
courtesy of Maree Gifkins*

CABAN / NO'J
The Trecena of Introspection

Caban, or No'j in K'iche' Maya, represents intelligence, ideas, wisdom, knowledge, and memory. It signifies dignity and honor, patience, prudence, and sublime, unconditional love; and also represents education, counseling, advising, meeting, and related activities. The nagual of intelligence, Caban invigorates the intellect and enriches the eternal quest for enlightenment. Just as time turns choice grapes into fine wine, so Caban turns knowledge and experience into wisdom. It is also the nagual of earthquakes and seismic disturbances, embodying the movement of earth and sky. Caban's animal totems are the woodpecker and the gazelle. In the Classical Maya tradition, it is associated with the cardinal direction East and the color red. In the tradition of modern-day K'iche' Maya, it is North and the color white. Caban is also one of the four Year Bearers, which shape the nature and character of the solar years they are associated with.

On Caban days, the Maya meet in council or in groups and ask for wisdom, talent, and the capacity to think positive, innovative, or productive thoughts or ideas. For the Maya, no one single person is wise; rather, it is the collective experience, knowledge, and insight of the group that create true wisdom. This is also a good day to ask for creativity in our endeavors, intelligence to address our challenges, and insight to resolve our issues. Indeed, Caban days are particularly propitious to ask for guidance from Mayan spiritual advisors, who may use the sacred *tz'ite* seeds to divine answers for our questions.

The trecena of Caban is ruled by the thoughtful, observant, introspective energy of this day sign. This is the time to use your powers of intellect and perception, of acuity and insight, and harness all that mental power for your personal growth, or help others to do so if that is your calling. The power of the human mind is unparalleled; there is nothing we cannot imagine, nothing we cannot achieve, nothing we cannot do.

But in order to empower the full depth and extent of your mental faculties, you need to dispel and disempower toxic forces such as fear, ego, greed, and malice—within yourself as well as influences coming in from the outside, from others. For these are the forces that monopolize your time, poison your thoughts, and undermine your actions. Indeed, these are the same forces that throughout history have prevented humanity from breaking the spell of slavery and attaining the higher, clearer mental frequencies necessary for enlightenment and evolution.

You will therefore need a significant amount of personal and mental freedom during the next thirteen days. Make room for you, for your soul, for your heart and mind. Clear your calendar, ask for more free time of your family or at work—and don't hesitate to take a day or two off, or a week if you can. Organize your bedroom, office or reading nook, and dedicate those times of the day that are naturally yours, to you and only you—whether it's dawn, late morning, afternoon, evening, or even late at night that you do your best work and think the most clearly. Only you know your natural inner rhythms, so honor your circadian time.

Also keep in mind that the greatest challenge of Caban is not to allow its acute sensitivities and powers of perception to bubble up into emotional upheavals, or to block you from living in the present moment. No use regretting or living in the past, or worrying about the future—those are simply more stagnant sentiments that will block your progress.

Once you have cleared away the physical and the psychic sources of chaos and clutter, you can focus on your mind, your intelligence and intellect. Regardless of how "unintellectual" you may feel or how "illogical" you may have been told you are, trust in your ability to reason and to think. It may take a little while to set those gears in motion, but as with any endeavor, practice makes perfect. You will be surprised how brilliantly you can think once your environment and your psyche are free and clear.

Trust your intelligence. Trust your instincts. Just be sure to keep them balanced, free and pure.

Hun (1) Caban
Jun (1) No'j

Start this trecena right: use the energy of One and the mental acuity of Caban to build a strong base for your thoughts and ideas. From thought arises will, from will desire, from desire action. Follow and flow with this current in full awareness of your capabilities and skills, but do not judge, do not compare, do not assess or value either the process or the result. Trust it and trust yourself. Retain patience deep within and you will have patience without. Remain balanced and in sync with your inner core; let not emotions, negative voices or the comments of others break the keel of your ship.

Enjoy the journey—you're here for the long haul.

Ka (2) Etznab
Kieb (2) Tijax

When Etznab rises in the trecena of Caban, you've got a powerful confluence of forces—the mental clarity of Caban is rendered ultra-sharp by Etznab's incisive insight and its unshakable perception of the difference between right and wrong, the line between truth and falsehood.

Be careful, however, not to wield this doubly powerful insight as a weapon or against others—it should be used as the gift that it truly is: a tool, a guide, a path to higher purpose.

Ox (3) Cauac
Oxib' (3) Kawoq

Like Ox (3) Imix, today is one of the most volatile days in the Tzolk'in. Cauac, the nagual of Water and Fire, of disputes, and the day sign of spiritual unrest and mental conflict, does not mix well with Ox's energies of uncertainty, insecurity, and risk. If you're not careful, today can whip up into a fierce hurricane of emotions or thoughts, or a mix of both, and send you reeling. But don't despair—call on the level-headed Caban, ruler of this trecena, to help you negotiate the churning storm Ox and Cauac are brewing overhead today.

Kan (4) Ahau
Kahib' (4) Ajpu

After the rain, the clouds part and sunlight breaks through. Whatever pain, whatever difficulties you may be going through now, remember they are as temporary as the bloom of a summer rose.

This trecena is about clearing your mental and physical space, for you. Today, let Ahau illuminate this new sacred space you're creating for yourself, shedding new light on old problems or situations, giving you a fresh, brilliant insight and vision for where you need to go or be.

Ho (5) Imix
Job' (5) Imox

Those who are able to connect to the beyond, to alternate realities, are either ahead or out of their time. Ho can take you to the many worlds of Imix faster than you think, so take a measured breath before you plunge in. To survive such a trip with your mind fully intact does take a fair amount of psychic strength and stability; luckily you have Caban's level-headed essence to ground you today as you explore different dimensions of your life, the questions or worries you may have, or possibilities for the kind of future you want to create.

Uac (6) Ik'
Wakib' (6) Iq'

O thou dreamers of fantastic flights, planners of big things, architects of alternate realities, let not the Wind disperse your blueprints or break apart the well-oiled engines that power your intentions. Harness instead this great force of nature that rides the wild horses within you, guide it with reason and knowing, and steady yourself to experience a higher level of achievement than you have heretofore lived.

This is also a day of cleansing and purification. Allow the winds of clarity to blow gently through your being, and with the centering energy of Uac, steady your soul back onto its true path.

Uuc (7) Akb'al
Wukub' (7) Aq'ab'al

When night falls and envelops all things in darkness, you need to attune your senses to navigate a different world. Things are not always what they seem: the sounds you hear, the things you see, the thoughts you think, are deeper, darker, more mysterious and magical, and colored by the absence of light. Use Caban's acute, cool-headed senses to guide your way through Akb'al's velvet depths. Above all, lose your fear and uncertainty along the way—for the Night is as glorious as the Day.

Uaxac (8) Kan
Wajxaqib' (8) K'at

Today is particularly auspicious for bringing abundance and fertility to fruition: Kan represents new offspring and the growth and increase of future generations, while Uaxac is one of the most sacred numbers for the Maya, holding the energy of wholeness and completion.

Together, Uaxac and Kan produce abundance in all of its forms, not only physical and financial resources: the abundance of love, of joy and enjoyment, of fresh ideas and new energy, of respect, honor and dignity, of free time and strong health. Open your self to these gifts!

Bolon (9) Chicchan
B'elejeb' (9) Kan

The Maya associated the number Nine with life and sacred ceremonies. Coupling Bolon with the intense energy of Chicchan produces a day extremely propitious for performing your personal rituals. Ask for vitality, clarity and an understanding of your soul's journey and purpose. Work on your physical, emotional, and spiritual strength by exercising your body and honoring its right to health, resolving personal or interpersonal issues and choosing happiness and joy, and dedicating time for meditation and inner silence.

Lahun (10) Cimi
Lajuj (10) Kame

The union of Lahun and Cimi yields a nurturing, healing energy that helps you to deepen your bonds with your loved ones, enrich your personal relationships, heal old wounds or misunderstandings, and improve any collaborations or cooperative endeavors you may be engaged in.

This is also a good day to reach out in meditation to your ancestors and learn from them and their lives. The bonds with our ancestors carry some of the most powerful forces in our lives—it is karma that runs in our blood, and it is we, the living, who must purify it.

Buluk (11) Manik'
Junlajuj (11) Kej

Focus is the key to today. Buluk's highly charged force increases
Manik's own power to make for an explosive combination, but that
requires clear, steady direction. Harnessed the right way, it can
help you accomplish a great deal today, or advance to the next level,
especially if you have personal issues to resolve.

Be sure, however, not to let today's intensity drive you to become
overbearing or domineering to others.

La Ka (12) Lamat
Kablajuj (12) Q'anil

This trecena has been all about using your intelligence, your acuity,
your rationality and insight. Lamat tempers this effort, letting us relax
a little and enjoy life. For it is not always in intense concentration,
hard work or research that the best ideas come to us—often it is, in
fact, in complete relaxation, when we're thinking about nothing at
all—this is that "letting go" we all talk about but are not so good
in actually doing. Try it today. Let go of your personal ambitions
and allow the natural abundance of the universe flow into your life
of its own accord.

Oxlahun (13) Muluc
Oxlajuj (13) Toj

When the profound currents of passion and purpose that define the human experience are guided with the highest grace and intention of the human mind, you attain the absolute in all that you seek. Today, receive the soft, flowing water and the rich, nurturing fire of Muluc, guided by the enhanced perception, intuition and spiritual insight of Oxlahun and tempered by the calm, cool Caban who rules this trecena, to bless the path of your personal progress to harmony and inner peace.

Oc / Tz'i
Ruler of the Trecena of Authority

original artwork, printed here in black & white,
courtesy of Maree Gifkins

OC / TZ'I
The Trecena of Authority

Oc, or Tz'i in K'iche' Maya, represents spiritual and material law and authority, justice and legality, and those who govern, determine, and enforce the law, such as lawmakers, lawyers, judges and magistrates, the police and other related professions. It also signifies fidelity, vengeance, order, accuracy, and precision. Oc is the nagual of sexuality and guides us to avoid the *Wuqub' Qak'ix*, the seven sins of ambition, pride, envy, lies, crime, ignorance, and ingratitude. The animal totems of Oc are the dog, the coyote, and the raccoon. In the Classical Maya tradition, it is associated with the cardinal direction North and the color white. In the tradition of modern-day K'iche' Maya, it is South and the color yellow.

On Oc days, the Maya ask for the ability to get rid of vices and to resolve the difficulties vices bring to their lives, and for solutions to legal issues and problems that are brought before the courts. This is a good day to be at peace and to pray that justice be granted to all people.

As we enter this trecena, let us reflect on the concepts of authority, justice, law and law enforcement and what that means, not just for each one of us individually, but for our society and civilization as a whole. Laws are designed by people for people, ideally to protect and support but also to control and restrict. And as with any other tool, the ultimate value and service of laws depend upon the intention with which they are created and how they are used. Justice—as opposed to a specific law—is a concept rather than a tool, and depends upon the perception of those who believe in it and the cultures which define it. So justice for one may not be justice for another. Authority, on the other hand, is a much more encompassing, and profound, power. It works with or without specific laws, written documents, or officials to enforce it. Legal authority is only one form of this power; in our society we also have political, business, medical, scientific, and many other types of authority. And above all of these, for many cultures and societies, including the Maya, is spiritual authority.

As you go through the Oc trecena, think about the authority that you exercise within your spheres of influence, whether it be at home, at work, in your social circles and local community, in the arts, sciences, the media or the public arena, or elsewhere. You may in fact hold different types and levels of authority in different circles. Consider how established your authority is, what is its source and where it comes from, and what it depends upon. Think about what you have been able to achieve as a direct impact of your authority, how you've improved others' lives as well as your own, how well you've prepared your children for life. What is the legacy you are leaving behind for future generations? Have you harmed anyone or anything in any way as a result of your authority, whether intentionally or not? If you have, think about how you can amend, assuage or reverse that harm, regardless of how long ago it may have taken place.

There is another type of authority and power that each and every human being holds, regardless of his or her position or rank in society. This is our role as stewards of the planet. We have the most advanced brain, the highest technology and science, the most complex language and social structures, and yet we wreak the greatest destruction all over our planet. In the world we have created, Nature has no "legal rights"—we kill, hunt, displace, or in some way directly or indirectly harm thousands of species every day, for food, research, entertainment, and sport, or simply out of negligence, and it's all an accepted part of our society. Without placing a moral judgment on modern societies, the fact is that our laws and concepts of justice are designed to govern and protect human beings, placing our desires and needs as an absolute priority above and over those of any other living thing on our planet.

We can turn this around, and use our resources and power for good. But it will take those of us whose authority has lain dormant, those of us who have wanted to do good but felt powerless, to wake up, stand up and claim the extraordinary power of our personal, spiritual, economic, and political authority to start changing the way human society interacts with the planet and its life-sustaining resources.

Above all, remember: the more authority you wield, the greater your responsibility in ensuring that power is used wisely and fairly.

Hun (1) Oc
Jun (1) Tz'i

On this first Oc or Tz'i day, lay the groundwork to awaken, strengthen and employ your personal authority for good or the betterment of others. The energy of Hun (One) is particularly important today, as it embodies the power of creation and inspiration—without which no idea, thought or intention would ever become reality. This is the energy you need to nourish your authority on whatever level and in whatever sphere you deem most fit and appropriate. The Maya perform ceremonies on Hun days; for this trecena, it is particularly important you do so as well.

Ka (2) Chuen
Kieb (2) B'atz'

Apart from all its wild antics, there is a more serious side to Chuen: this is the most propitious day sign for marriage. Today is particularly auspicious, as Chuen walks hand in hand with Ka (Two), the number of duality, of the yin and the yang. If you're planning a wedding, anniversary, or engagement, set it for Ka Chuen. If that's not a possibility, any Chuen day will do just fine.

Even if there is no one special in your life at the moment, today is a highly auspicious day to ask for him or her to come into your life.

Ox (3) Eb
Oxib' (3) E'

We all travel along our individual lifepaths, in each lifetime, only once. And because Time doesn't give second chances, it's important not only to make the best and most informed choices we possibly can, but also to avoid wasting precious moments on negative, stagnant or toxic emotions and energies. Look down the long, vast horizon of your personal path that Eb unveils for you today, and do so with confidence, faith and courage. You'll need it to ward off Ox's propensity toward doubt and uncertainty.

Kan (4) Ben
Kahib' (4) Aj

The home is the ultimate school: this is where we are brought up, where we learn more about life than anywhere else, where our identity and understanding of the world and human relationships are shaped. But home is also within us—the emotional or psychic home, the spiritual or soul home where the core of our being resides. It is this cross-blending of homes that makes us complete; and certainly none of them would in turn be complete without tenderness and compassion balanced with responsibility, practicality, and life experience.

Ho (5) Ix
Job' (5) I'x

The Jaguar knows how to lie in wait until the decisive moment of action arrives. Patiently, biding his time, sensing the movement of the air and the leaves of the trees, the pitter patter of the ants underfoot... If you walk in silence, think without speaking, act without agendas, you will reap the harvest of your intentions ahead of those who rush clamoring to attract attention. And the fruits of your effort will last much longer.

Uac (6) Men
Wakib' (6) Tz'ikin

Even the sacred Tzolk'in has a little humor built in... today, quite literally, "the Eagle has landed!" Men, the Eagle, soars high into the stratosphere to give you acute clarity and insight into your personal circumstances, relationships, troubles and questions. If you're not used to such heights, rely on the four-fold stabilizing energy of Uac to land your flight on solid ground.

Uuc (7) Cib
Wukub' (7) Ajmaq

Philosophers from ancient times used to say we don't learn new things, we just remember what we always knew. With today's vertiginous rate of change and progress, there certainly always seem to be new things to learn—and as soon as we learn them, they have all changed and become obsolete. But this is not the kind of knowledge the ancients were referring to... deep inside we are all timeless souls who know the profound truths of human life.

Honor your ancient soul today.

Uaxac (8) Caban
Wajxaqib' (8) No'j

When you are engaged in any kind of team or collaborative activity, whether you're having dinner with friends or family, solving a problem at work with colleagues, or playing beach volleyball, it is often the quiet side, the introspective, grounded mind that brings new perspectives to any conversation or situation.

Too often in our society, it's about who talks the most or the loudest—but give voice to the apparently timid and you may be surprised!

Bolon (9) Etznab
B'elejeb' (9) Tijax

A great day for oration, especially if you are to speak at a family or social event—be it birthdays, weddings and engagement announcements, graduation parties, religious ceremonies or rites of passage, or funerals. Even if you are the most timid of public speakers, take heart in the powerful support and encouragement you receive today from Etznab, which enhances your communication capabilities, and Bolon, which is highly auspicious for important events and occasions. If you are planning an event for or with your family or loved ones, today is a good day—particularly if the event includes a toast or a speech.

Lahun (10) Cauac
Lajuj (10) Kawoq

The highest epitome of teamwork, the droplets of Cauac's powerful energies fall to the ground in a highly organic and chaotic, yet structured and cohesive dance, an orchestra of collaboration that results in some of nature's most wondrous magic. Today, dance with those who are your closest, most natural raindrops... and be ready to receive the blessings and unexpected rewards of your collective cooperation.

Buluk (11) Ahau
Junlajuj (11) Ajpu

As an arrow shot from the trained bow of Ahau and guided by the sharp vision of Oc, Buluk gathers enormous speed and power as it flies toward its target. Neither positive nor negative, it doesn't judge or compare, but brings awe-inspiring force to whatever it is you focus on today. It is therefore up to you to lead, to give today's energy direction, focus and purpose. Choose carefully. Will you steer your lifepath away from rage, enmity and malice, toward success, enlightenment and wisdom in your personal challenges and difficulties?

La Ka (12) Imix
Kablajuj (12) Imox

It's all relative, as they say. What you do or say today may have a completely unexpected impact or effect tomorrow. So before you judge, before you regret anything you've done or said in your life, reconsider and rethink it in the context of your overall lifetime rather than a given moment of reference. Of all the numbers of the Tzolk'in, La Ka knows how to navigate the chaotic waters of Imix; heed its advice to put everything into the larger perspective—whether that of your individual lifetime, generational, societal, cultural or historical.

Oxlahun (13) Ik'
Oxlajuj (13) Iq'

Oxlahun powers up the winds of Ik', driving their energy to extraordinary strength. Don't fight or fear this force—take it on, embody it, become fully one with it, and allow it to empower your personal authority to do good in whatever form and wherever it is needed, whether for your community, country, family, or very simply, for yourself.

Akb'al / Aq'ab'al
Ruler of the Trecena of Potential

original artwork, printed here in black & white,
courtesy of Maree Gifkins

AKB'AL / AQ'AB'AL
The Trecena of Potential

A kb'al, or Aq'ab'al in K'iche' Maya, symbolizes both darkness and dawn, those magical times of the day when Night cedes to Day and Day gives way to Night. These are periods of transition, of grace, of potential—and polarity, which Akb'al naturally embodies. It is light and dark, heat and cold, opposing sides and opposite energies. Akb'al embodies the essence of the love between a man and a woman, of marriage, romance and all matters of physical, spiritual, and emotional love. It also signifies harmony, truth, hope and solemnity; awakening and enchantment; magical spells, mystery and devotion. It is the nagual of clarity and light, a force of renewal, and helps us gain illumination into the issues that impact our lives. The animal totems of Akb'al are the fawn and the macaw. In the Classical Maya tradition, it is associated with the cardinal direction West and the color black. In the tradition of modern-day K'iche' Maya, it is East and the color red.

On Akb'al days, the Maya ask for a wife or husband, for this day sign is the most propitious of them all for love, romance and marriage. It is equally customary to ask for humility and blessings. Akb'al days can also be very favorable for securing employment.

This is the realm of Night, of the great deep Void where nothing yet exists and all potential dwells. This is the place where all things begin, all roads commence, all thoughts germinate; and the place where everything ends, all paths converge, and the ultimate impact of all intentions becomes material.

For all beginnings are endings on the other side of their reality, and all endings bloom yet again in a burst of renewed energy and life—these are the sacred cycles of existence, large, small, microscopic and too boundless to enumerate, cycles that pulsate in infinite variety and on infinite levels of complexity, repeated and iterated in every droplet of consciousness as well as the great unconscious... cycles that we, the human species, endeavor to explain by fragmenting them into a million multicolored pieces that our minds can grasp.

Fulfilling your potential is really a matter of awareness, of acceptance, of letting go. To be aware is to know yourself fully, on all levels and in all aspects of your being; for without awareness you cannot begin to understand your true potential. To accept is to love you and who you are, without preconditions, judgments or comparisons, and to extend this love to others no matter how stinging their criticisms of you, no matter how sharp their tongues, no matter how intolerant their views, for they in turn may not yet be ready to accept and love themselves. To let go is to respect and trust in yourself and your chosen lifepath, and to release toxic emotions, thoughts, and attitudes, whether your own or those of others, that would fracture your life's horizon.

In times of despair, uncertainty, or fear, remember that fulfilling your potential is both the toughest and the simplest thing you'll ever do. Yes, you are indeed free to choose which path to follow, which direction in life to take, which aspects of your soul to let bloom, but it may take a lifetime to figure it all out—and often does. But before you can choose, you need to be aware that choices exist at all—many cultures, religions, and family environments shackle their people with rules, customs, and laws that depress or prevent the realization of individual potential. You must first break free of your prisons and forgive those who put you there, before you can learn how to fly.

Honor the sacred seed of potential that is your soul... sink into the profound, pregnant silence of Akb'al and release all earthly stresses, pressures and deadlines. For here, time has no sway. Here, all simply is, was, and will be. This is where the core of all things vibrates into existence, bathed in an inner peace that has neither beginning nor end, holding within the possibility to become anything and to be everything. This, too, is you.

Hun (1) Akb'al
Jun (1) Aq'ab'al

Honor your sleep today. Sleep is the time when your mind, body and soul regenerate, refresh and rejuvenate. So if this day falls on a weekend, sleep in as long as you can, to let that sweet rest wash over and through your entire being. If it's a weekday, you might rise earlier to be with the dawn at her first breath—not to get extra work done, but to honor that first kiss of the day, brimming with potential and promise. In both cases, awaken profoundly refreshed.

Ka (2) Kan
Kieb (2) K'at

Any tool, object or concept can be used for good or for evil: a knife can slice vegetables for a meal or it can kill; money can provide needed resources or it can corrupt; competition can drive healthy progress or it can destroy relationships. This is the inherent duality in all things and all aspects of life. What makes the difference? Intention. That is Kan's and Ka's challenge to you today: will you cast Kan's net so that you can provide fish for your entire village, or only hoard the catch for yourself? Will you free yourself of the people or situations holding you down, or continue to suffer? The answer may seem obvious on paper, but in real life it may not be quite as simple to do. Choose wisely.

Ox (3) Chicchan
Oxib' (3) Kan

Pure potential carries no value. It's not right, it's not wrong, it's not black and it's not white. Today, Chicchan's ancestral fire ignites Akb'al's seeds, breaking them open into a dazzling burst of possibilities. Better keep your distance, however, for Ox brings in highly variable winds that can scatter these brilliant sparks in any direction, and anything you undertake could turn out for the worse just as easily as it can succeed. If you can hold off on any material decisions or active plans, you will retain today's powerful energies for a better day.

Kan (4) Cimi
Kahib' (4) Kame

Connect with your family and your ancestors, both the living and those who lived before, to understand the path you now walk. Buried in your personal lineage are insights, lessons, and illuminations that can explain and clarify more than you would imagine about the events, people and situations in your present lifetime. Listen to these messages coming to you from life and the beyond, and let Kan's stabilizing energies ground your soul in the bedrock of ancient wisdom and life experience.

Ho (5) Manik'
Job' (5) Kej

Rise at dawn and walk alone to honor your innate strength and power, look far into the horizon to foresee events that will impact you or require your influence, breath deep to take in the early scent of things to come. Ride with Ho into the morning light to catch those early bursts of energy. Whatever your role or purpose in life, respect and honor it today, and commit your mind, body and soul with clarity of intention, nobility of spirit, and strength of will.

Uac (6) Lamat
Wakib' (6) Q'anil

It is at night, the embodiment of pregnant silence, the depths of the ocean, the quiet of our souls, that new life begins: the germination of ideas, innovations, discoveries, empires, and yes... of new life. Bathed by the rich currents of potential of Akb'al, Lamat blooms into an ocean of infinite possibility that is yours to nurture, nourish and realize.

Honor the sanctity of your night.

Uuc (7) Muluc
Wukub' (7) Toj

Direct the currents of energy and emotion in your life and your heart as a canyon directs a raging river: one carves the other, yet the other steers the one. For the power of Muluc, like any other great power, must be used with great responsibility, humility, and care. Uuc brings in a full 360 degrees of possibility that you can apply to whatever part of your life you need it most. The key lies in knowing how, when and where to apply these energies, and on what scale or level. If you keep your intentions pure and your gratitude for your karmic path sincere, you will be able to steer Uuc and Muluc toward your chosen horizon.

Uaxac (8) Oc
Wajxaqib' (8) Tz'i

Today gives you clarity of thought and perception as you seek to resolve difficulties and challenges in your life, or perhaps vices or bad habits you are aware of and wish to dispel and clear away. The energy of Uaxac is especially propitious for completing cycles of cleansing, soul searching and spiritual enlightenment, and will be greatly intensified with ritual or ceremony.

Bolon (9) Chuen
B'elejeb' (9) B'atz'

An absolutely blessed day for marriage, weddings, and the conception of children. Bolon, the "number of life," interlaces its life-giving energies through Chuen's rich tapestry of living consciousness to produce a psychic environment pulsing with profound potential.

Do not take this day for granted. Honor and respect it for the extraordinary and sacred power it holds for your union in love.

Lahun (10) Eb
Lajuj (10) E'

The road you travel by day is not the same path you take by night. Open your heart to one and you will open a path for many. Serve as a guiding light for those just starting their journey, so that others may in turn guide you. Invite those you hold dearest to travel your path with you, and your horizon will open up to the heavens. The more roads we can connect and link with others, the more travelers can come together and mutually enrich their journeys. Some may choose the solitary path, but even the lone traveler will find comfort in the company of friends and loved ones, no matter for how brief a time their paths should cross.

Buluk (11) Ben
Junlajuj (11) Aj

Ben carries an intense connection with home and family; in the context of Akb'al, symbolizing the potential inherent in all things, this connection deepens further. Buluk takes this intensity sky-high, off the charts, pulling in the totality of all aspects of your home and family life—past, present and future.

And because Buluk doesn't take sides, this can materialize in either highly positive or highly negative outcomes, so take care not to make hasty or overly emotional decisions. Let things play out and remember those closest to you... are the closest to you.

La Ka (12) Ix
Kablajuj (12) I'x

Learn from Ix the Jaguar's stealth, patience and deep understanding of the jungle, and you will hear the softer voices of living things that the tumult of machines and men drown out. If you quiet your own chattering voices, stop your trains of thought, and step off the treadmill of modern life, even for a few moments each day in meditation, you will gain greater, deeper insight into who you are, what your purpose in this lifetime is, and what external influences— be it family, work, society or culture—are derailing your path.

Oxlahun (13) Men
Oxlajuj (13) Tz'ikin

Today presents one of the most powerful days in the Tzolk'in for acute, piercing perception into the depths of your soul, for getting clarity on long-sitting issues you have not been able to resolve, and for seeing far into the long, long horizon of your life path. The intensity of insight can be so great that it can blind, stun and paralyze—so as you soar with Oxlahun and Men today, keep an open and non judgmental mind and spirit; make no decisions and take no actions until you've come back down to ground level and had time to process what you've seen.

CIB / AJMAQ
RULER OF THE TRECENA
OF WISDOM AND FORGIVENESS

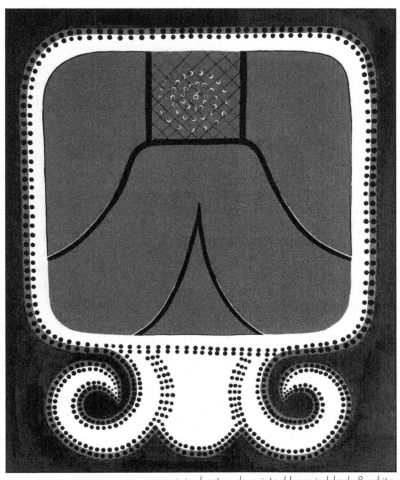

*original artwork, printed here in black & white,
courtesy of Maree Gifkins*

CIB / AJMAQ
The Trecena of Wisdom and Forgiveness

Cib, or Ajmaq in K'iche' Maya, represents the wisdom and the souls of our ancestors, of the ancients that came before us, both in our own bloodline and in the human family now inhabiting the Earth. The energy of Cib embodies our connection to the long history of life through evolution, through the millions of years that have elapsed and blessed our planet with the diversity of life we see today, and the sanctity of consciousness, free will and love. Cib also represents forgiveness, pardon, sin, and pleasure. It is the nagual of all faults and vices. But it also symbolizes gifts and Mother Earth, and is the nagual of the Earth itself. The animal totems of Cib are the vulture and the owl. In the Classical Maya tradition, it is associated with the cardinal direction South and the color yellow. In the tradition of modern-day K'iche' Maya, it is West and the color black.

On Cib days, the Maya ask for forgiveness from their ancestors, for this is the time when they are listening and are favorably predisposed to hear our wishes and requests. This is also a good day to manage harmony and discord. In the Classical Period, Cib helped the Maya maintain balance in their lives: it was a day to stay home and reflect on one's acts and their consequences, be they intentional or not.

Cib embodies two archetypal energies: forgiveness and wisdom. Forgiveness has been written about a lot in the popular press lately, perhaps because we need it more than ever. The high rates of divorce, lawsuits, and crime related to hate, envy, vendettas, and other interpersonal issues that mark societies in many "developed" nations, are the symptom of our inability, or unwillingness, to forgive. Forgiveness carries with it a vast ocean of powerful forces: love, respect, integrity, honor, compassion, understanding, and empathy. Until you are able to forgive, fully, completely, and unconditionally, until you are able to stop seeking vengeance or revenge, you are not truly free. You are still under the control of the person who has wronged you, for you dedicate your thoughts, emotions and energy to them. First and foremost, you must forgive yourself, and that may be yet more difficult than pardoning others. Many of us carry deep-seated guilt, sometimes without knowing it. That guilt, whatever its roots, must come out.

When you forgive, you let go, you release and liberate. Not only those who may have wronged you, but more importantly, yourself. And that is the greatest gift you can give to yourself and those around you.

Cib also embodies the experience of wisdom and insight gained through the experience of long life. For the Maya, attaining the status of Elder, which occurs at 52 years of age—when you have completed 4 cycles of 13 years each—is one of the highest accomplishments of a human being. Ironically, modern Western society worships the vigor and idealism of youth, and treats its elders as no longer productive or useful. They are considered a burden rather than the treasures of wisdom they really are. This is critical, because unless we respect and recognize the priceless knowledge and experience that our elders carry, we will continue to be doomed to repeat the errors and ill-advised decisions of the past—and this applies to all levels and aspects of our society, from foreign policy and economic indicators to our own social values and professional success. Our elders are our only link to what came before us, our only connection to past generations and their hard-learned lessons. No books, no web sites, no global social network can replace the profound living wisdom our elders embody. Cutting off these vital lines severs us from our own collective consciousness and prevents us from moving forward individually and as a society.

This is why connecting to the paths the ancestors have walked is so crucial. Not just your direct bloodline, but also all those who came before you, whose learning, work, and efforts you are now enjoying in the form of all the technologies, techniques, processes, inventions, and other tools and knowledge that make your life more productive, convenient, and enjoyable.

Reconnect with the elders, both living and passed on, and you will reconnect with your own soul.

Hun (1) Cib
Jun (1) Ajmaq

If this is the first time you're considering the possibility of forgiveness in your life, whether for yourself or for someone who has wronged you, go forward! Rest assured you are supported by the positive, initiating energy of Hun. When an idea enters your waking awareness, it announces its readiness to materialize and become reality. And there are few things more healing or more liberating, for all those whom it touches, than forgiveness.

Ka (2) Caban
Kieb (2) No'j

Honor the duality of reason and inspiration, of thought and emotion, of the physical and the spiritual, of the active and the passive. Honor the sacred process of creating thought, ideas, and awareness, for it is all linked to your karmic destiny, patterns of perception and insights of interpretation, these threads of living energy spinning from an ancient past into an effervescent future that only you design. Connect to that part of your soul that speaks to the ancestors and seeks to understand the wisdom they are giving you.

Ox (3) Etznab
Oxib' (3) Tijax

There is a reason for the expression "double-edged sword." When you balance on the edge of one, all you need to fall to one side is a slight nudge. You therefore need to be especially careful today, for Ox can turn Etznab from a tool of truth and healing into a weapon of vengeance, falsehood and poison. Luckily you've got Cib's trecena on your side, which will help you navigate Ox's churning energies. Use today not to start something new or venture into unknown territory of any kind, but to seek balance and harmony, and to purify your thoughts.

Kan (4) Cauac
Kahib' (4) Kawoq

Where are rainstorms born? Some are born of the breath of ancient forests, some of the tears of the wind; some germinate in the warm moist bosom of the tropics, others percolate down from the frozen North... whereever your personal rainstorm begins, that's where your journey starts. Seek the birthplace of your rainstorm and you shall understand the source of your soul.

Ho (5) Ahau
Job' (5) Ajpu

Whatever your personal challenge or conflict, foresight and anticipation are weapons worth their weight in gold. If you rise early and attune to the morning winds borne on Ho's outstretched wings, you'll foresee and foresense the right path out of difficulty, perhaps even before it materializes. How many times do we make mistakes or say things we later regret! We cannot go back in time to fix things, but we can learn to anticipate.

Indeed, some of the world's deadliest martial arts follow this golden principle of evasion: if you can anticipate, you can avoid. If you can avoid, you live longer.

Uac (6) Imix
Wakib' (6) Imox

Uac and Imix are not the most well-matched of partners—or the greatest of friends. Imix opens the doors to alternate realities and "other" dimensions, while Uac is fairly intolerant of anything but the most practical, no-nonsense approach to any aspect of life. So you may go through or receive some conflicting—and perhaps even a little maddening—experiences, viewpoints or advice that you will need to sift through on your own. And yet... not completely on your own. We are in the trecena of Cib, which carries the wisdom of the ancestors, so you might want to reach out through your bloodline to anchor yourself as you process today's energies.

Uuc (7) Ik'
Wukub' (7) Iq'

Uuc on an Ik' day is risky. Wind can turn on a dime, and with Uuc, the middle number of the Tzolk'in, this indecisiveness is only magnified. If you're going through a challenging or emotionally taxing period in your life, take extra time to think through any action or steps you plan to take to resolve the situation—and take solace in the underlying current of Cib, which soothes you with forgiveness and compassion.

Otherwise, feel free to play with the multiple perspectives that Uuc affords you, and harness Ik's force toward the one you want to take!

Uaxac (8) Akb'al
Wajxaqib' (8) Aq'ab'al

Walk the path of your ancestors guided by the profound, silent energy of Akb'al. Connect to the mysteries that have led your soul along a timeless journey into your present lifetime, and pull your future through the light of the coming dawn. Quiet the mind as you meditate, seek out that spacetime of your being that contains the seeds of all of your possibilities, your dreams, thoughts and intentions, and bring them forth to your conscious experience so that they may clarify and guide your life's purpose once again.

Bolon (9) Kan
B'elejeb' (9) K'at

Our sexual drive is one of the most powerful, primal forces in the human experience. Religions have tried to subvert it; cultures and societies have tried to control it; military initiatives have used it as a weapon of war. To this day, the human sexual force is misused, abused, and overconsumed. Today, and henceforward, release the guilt and the shame, the lust and the decadence, as well as the denial and the abstention. Let go of all the labels and judgments, and honor this sacred force for what it really is: the purest, most ancient and life-giving primal power that we human beings have been blessed with. Honor and respect it for the rest of your life.

Lahun (10) Chicchan
Lajuj (10) Kan

Chicchan, the great feathered serpent and the nagual of the sexual union between woman and man, winds sensuously around Lahun's social and familial energies, while Lahun harmonizes Chicchan's burning inner fire. Their pairing breathes life into a union of energies that parallels the coupling of the male and female essence, the sacred and passionate bond between man and woman that creates new human life.

What else need be said? Surrender yourself today!

Buluk (11) Cimi
Junlajuj (11) Kame

Flow with the endless cycles and transformations of life, whether great or small, all-encompassing or incidental; watch, observe and allow them to work through your soul. Resist the temptation to judge, control or make assumptions, for they will take all that much longer to resolve. Buluk's power is too strong and too high minded to be swayed by the petty perspectives that too often influence us. It is best to let go, trust in the awesome presence of Buluk and Cimi, and focus on the great vast horizon that is your destiny.

La Ka (12) Manik'
Kablajuj (12) Kej

When you attain knowledge or understanding of something, it is your right and duty to speak up and stand for what is right and what is true. But have your facts straight before you do so, for in today's world, disinformation and misinformation abound in ever greater volumes: on the Internet, television, media and advertising. Draw upon La Ka's low-frequency resonance with the currents that underlie your life, and, regardless of your age, embody the elder within you. Walk that calm, steady inner path, for that is where true power lies.

Oxlahun (13) Lamat
Oxlajuj (13) Q'anil

As we enter this last day of the Cib trecena, honor the journey you have made: honor the wisdom and advice of your ancestors, honor and keep it in your heart for the rest of your life. Oxlahun seals this learning with the voluminous abundance of Lamat, amplifying its impact and effects multifold throughout all aspects of your life. From here on, you carry with you vast oceans of knowledge, experience and wisdom that you can call upon at any time.

Take care, however, not to squander the wisdom and insights you have gained—use them well and use them for a good purpose.

Muluc / Toj
Ruler of the Trecena of Harmony

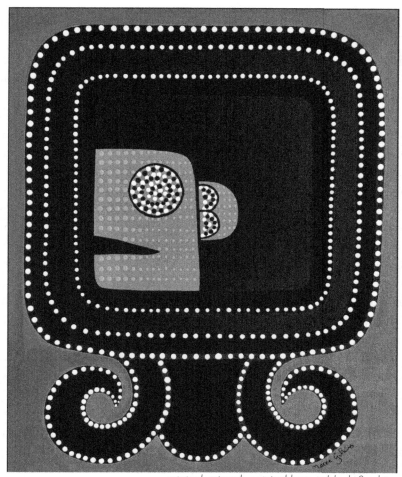

original artwork, printed here in black & white,
courtesy of Maree Gifkins

MULUC / TOJ
The Trecena of Harmony

A sign of harmony, balance, and equilibrium, Muluc, or Toj in K'iche' Maya, embodies not only the power, freedom, and inner peace that these states of grace carry, but also all of the struggles and challenges we go through to achieve and maintain them in our lives. It is, in a word, the sign of karma, the sign of payment and the energy of the law of action and reaction that the concept of karma carries. A potent and highly charged sign, Muluc packs a powerful swell of energies that can sweep you off your feet at any moment. It has the unique distinction of being the nagual of two primal elements, Water and Fire, in its manifestation of rain and in its embodiment of the sacred fire in Maya fire ceremonies, respectively. It also represents offering, payment, fines, and debt; and signifies such emotionally heavy concepts as carnal pleasures, ill omens, child abuse and neglect, and spousal abuse. The animal totems of Muluc are the shark and the puma. In the Classical Maya tradition, it is associated with the cardinal direction East and the color red. In the tradition of modern-day K'iche' Maya, it is North and the color white.

On Muluc days, the Maya give thanks for everything that has come into their lives, regardless of its moral value. On this day, we should acknowledge our karmic debt with humility and sincerity, and assert our intention to reconcile that debt by achieving balance and harmony in our lives. We should also express gratitude for all that is in balance and atone for any disequilibrium still remaining. This is a good day to settle, pay or reconcile debts in general, not just karmic: they may be financial, moral or personal.

This trecena, strive to achieve complete and total balance, equilibrium, and harmony. Regardless of how close you actually get to this goal, it is the intention and the journey that bring the greatest benefit, for in setting these states of grace as your horizon, you open your soul to their healing, calming energies. This is, in fact, the secret path to resolving and balancing the karma you hold, whether it's karma that you bring into this lifetime or that you have accumulated over the years. Resist the temptation to right wrongs done to you, teach someone "a lesson," hold grudges, or pay someone back for unfair or unethical treatment or an act of malice. Remember that whoever has wronged you, has in fact built negative karma against themselves, typically in direct proportion and intensity to the act in question; therefore it is not necessary for you to expend effort in trying to balance the charges. In fact, you may generate your own negative karma if you do engage in some form of vengeance, thus producing an infinite loop of retaliation that ultimately serves no one.

Flow instead with a higher spiritual current: stay with the energy of forgiveness that the previous trecena imparted to you, and continue to learn to forgive and let go, and release yourself from the binding, toxic energies of revenge and retribution. This is a powerful way to liberate yourself from the past and set a magnificent example for all who come into your sphere of influence. Not only will you humble and inspire those who've wronged you, but also possibly inspire others to follow the same path to harmony instead of submitting to retaliation.

Since Muluc is the nagual of both water and fire, two primal forces, it is a good practice throughout this trecena to honor them both in some way: light a candle at the beginning or end—or both—of each of its thirteen days, meditate at sunrise when the light is brightest, take a relaxing bath, drink plenty of pure water.

If you are a Muluc by birth or nature, this trecena will bring out your innate essence and resonate with your powerful currents of emotion and intelligence. You may have noticed throughout your life that your intensity, flexibility, and the ability to adapt to almost any situation or change at a moment's notice, causes mistrust or misunderstanding in others who are not quite so adaptable or emotionally charged. If this is the case, you might use the energy of Muluc to carve out channels of communication that you may not have tried before that will more easily and effectively reach your loved ones, friends, and colleagues.

Hun (1) Muluc
Jun (1) Toj

Give thanks for all that is part of your life, all that has come in and all that has yet to arrive, without placing judgment or assigning moral value. Acknowledge your karmic debt that you have accumulated over the years and set the intention to reconcile it with humility and sincerity.

Hun empowers Muluc today with a powerful impetus, so that Muluc's energies may last you the entire trecena. Flow with it, strive not to control it, honor its depth and its power, let it go and let it work its natural magic for you.

Ka (2) Oc
Kieb (2) Tz'i

Do not seek vengeance for the wrongs that have been done to you, lest you become caught in an infinite game of payback. Flow with a higher spiritual current: learn instead to forgive and let go, and release yourself from the binding, toxic energies of 'teaching someone a lesson'. You will set a far greater example for those who've wronged you through forgiveness and understanding.

Ox (3) Chuen
Oxib' (3) B'atz'

Handle with care! This is one of the riskiest days in the Tzolk'in. Chuen's boisterous energy, coupled with the propensity of Ox to haul in risk, doubt, and uncertainty, strews rocks, bales of hay, and random airplane parts all over today's energetic landscape. But if you enjoy—or even thrive on—unpredictability, chaos, and serendipity, today may deliver the kind of thrills you seek. Just be warned: plunge in at your own risk!

Kan (4) Eb
Kahib' (4) E'

The stronger and more stable your inner core and foundation, the brighter your path and the wider your horizon. Use the undercurrent of Muluc in this trecena to harmonize your life by acknowledging your karmic debts as a natural part of your life's journey. Give thanks to Eb for sustaining and illuminating your journey, and call on the four-fold stabilizing energy of Kan to guide you toward the fulfillment of your intended destiny.

Ho (5) Ben
Job' (5) Aj

As a reed in flowing water bends, so too should we ebb and flow with the tides of each day we live, each person we meet, each conversation we share. These natural currents of the waking experience of life enrich our consciousness and keep our homes humming. Sink into the rhythms that are natural to you, and don't try to anticipate or speed up anything, especially if you feel driven by what your neighbors or other family members are doing.

Uac (6) Ix
Wakib' (6) I'x

No matter your dreams and fantasies, your longings and what-if scenarios, the only way to achieve anything in life is through focus, commitment, discipline and a practical approach to challenges and difficulties. The Jaguar doesn't float on thin air; he is grounded, connected to the real world, ever vigilant and ever aware of everything around him. His faculties of smell, sight and his acute natural instinct guide his sure-footed progress to attaining his goals.

Dream to achieve, not to escape.

Uuc (7) Men
Wukub' (7) Tz'ikin

As above, so below. Men, the Eagle, soars above the powerful currents of Muluc, and they in turn reflect his path. Let your higher self, not your ego, guide the currents of your heart, and in turn your heart shall fulfill the intentions of your higher soul.

Your challenge is to handle the all-seeing Uuc, which can impart too many perspectives and too many angles as you travel along your path. Stay balanced and confident, trust your higher self.

Uaxac (8) Cib
Wajxaqib' (8) Ajmaq

Cib and Muluc were born for each other. Intertwined the act and sentiment of forgiveness and the desire and intent for karmic equilibrium, cradled in the strong, steady arms of Uaxac, today is one of the most powerful days in the Tzolk'in for karmic and personal atonement for all disharmony and imbalance, all sins or crimes committed, all wrongs perpetrated. Connect with your ancestors and your own soul, and make a promise to you and your soul line that you shall seek harmony and karmic state of grace.

Bolon (9) Caban
B'elejeb' (9) No'j

Following on the heels of Cib, Caban also has a connection to the Earth and to ancient wisdom. Take a moment to step away, even if it's just in your mind, from our modern society's frenetic rhythm and mentality, from our collective anxieties and fears, and remember that we still have a slower, more natural world all around us that's ready to soothe us the moment we choose to notice it.

Lahun (10) Etznab
Lajuj (10) Tijax

Ever try to capture a fast-moving river current? Etznab has that razor-sharp capacity of insight that acts like sonar to penetrate the most turbulent problems, issues, or situations you may find yourself in, give you clarity and insight, and help heal emotional or psychic wounds. To aid the process along, Lahun brings in the elements of cooperation and bonding to strengthen relationships among the people in your life. Trust Lahun and Etznab in your energetic space right now and the waters will, as they say in a well-known ancient text, part for you.

Buluk (11) Cauac
Junlajuj (11) Kawoq

Whatever imbalance or disequilibrium there may be in your life right now, it is neither permanent nor immutable. To you, things might feel heavy and set in stone, impossible to move or change, but there is nothing that can withstand the overwhelming force of water once released. So seize the untamed power of Buluk and let the cleansing, purifying energies of Cauac wash away the troubles weighing down your soul, clear you of the emotional poison smeared upon you by others, and free you of the mental and physical prisons you yourself have built.

La Ka (12) Ahau
Kablajuj (12) Ajpu

La Ka lays out all of the struggles, challenges and conflicts, as well as all of the insights and moments of leadership you've experienced thus far in your life. Ahau's burning gaze pours unforgiving light onto it all... it can be quite a humbling experience. But if you are sincere with yourself and accept responsibility for your role in these events without self-judgment, and acknowledge your karmic debt without guilt, you will be able to rebalance and place your lifepath back in harmony with the purpose of your higher soul.

Oxlahun (13) Imix
Oxlajuj (13) Imox

Oxlahun is the numerical soulmate of Imix. They both carry the ability to access other dimensions and realities; they are both highly charged, powerful signs. Paired together, they form a veritable vortex of mind-bending energies that can spin psychic tornados around your soul. Be warned! If you do venture into their world today, the realm of the unknown, the undreamed, don't go in without a lifeline. Indeed, Muluc, the ruler of this trecena, may be the only thing to help steady your ship as you head into these raging waters.

Ik' / Iq'
Ruler of the Trecena of Communication

*original artwork, printed here in black & white,
courtesy of Maree Gifkins*

IK' / IQ'
The Trecena of Communication

Ik', or Iq' in K'iche' Maya, represents the wind and the air in all of its forms, from warm tropical breezes to ocean zephyrs, from crackling lightning and thunder to fierce howling hurricanes. This is the wind that sweeps clean the heart and psyche, the body and mind. This is the breath of life that heals all negative energy and illness, be it of a physical or psychological nature, but especially if the problem stems from anger or rage. It's the energy of words and communication, the conception and expression of ideas. A day sign of cleansing and purification, Ik' is the nagual of the moon and the air, of the divine breath and vital spirit of human existence. Yet it also signifies crisis, suffering and grief, asphyxiation, sexual perversion, and failure. Ik' symbolizes the purity and translucence of glass, and graphically represents the T-shaped windows of Mayan temples, which served the dual purpose of determining what kind of wind was blowing by the sound it made through the window, and observing astronomical phenomena and movements of stars and planets. The animal totems of Ik' are the bobcat, weasel, and hummingbird. In the Classical Maya tradition, it is associated with the cardinal direction North and the color white. In the tradition of modern-day K'iche' Maya, it is South and the color yellow. Ik' is also one of the four Year Bearers, which shape the nature and character of the solar years they are associated with.

On Ik' days, the Maya ask for the strength, vital energy, perseverance, and commitment to fulfill their life's purpose and chosen profession. This is a good day to ask for renewal and fresh winds to purify and inspire our minds, or strengthen our mental powers. Ik' days are also excellent for healing psychological problems and for cleansing ourselves of negative passions, sentiments, and depressions.

For the Maya, the power of communication is the highest differentiator between the human race and other living beings; to be eloquent in our prayers and words is therefore the greatest gift we can bestow upon one another. It is a gift that is little appreciated today, and perhaps all the more reason to remind ourselves of the power and impact of the spoken and written word, and the responsibility of integrity and honor we all bear when we promise something to someone, express our opinions, or argue for or against something.

Communication can be verbal, visual, auditory, kinetic, sensual, emotional, psychic, or spiritual. However you express yourself, to communicate is, in its simplest form, to be connected. In the modern world, to be connected does not mean spending your life on social networks or your smartphone. It means to be actively present, in your mind, body and soul, and to be aware of others, other living beings, the natural environment, your family and community, and yourself. Regardless of whether you're a poet or can barely put an email together, if you quiet the nonstop media machine we're all plugged into, you'll be able to tune into the finer, subtler frequencies of real human communication, which vibrates at a much higher and deeper level.

Ik', the Wind, is the breath of spirit and of life, in endless motion and endless movement, climbing miles into the stratosphere and pulling back down again, skipping across altitudes, blowing hot or freezing cold, whipping up fierce storms and lolling balmy breezes. Ironically, Wind is as fickle as it is strong—it can change direction on a moment's notice, or gust to a tornado from a mild breeze. But if you are aware and tuned in, you will notice those signs and hints of change that can be short-lived—ephemeral in fact—but tell of major shifts to come.

The Wind also cleanses and purifies, sweeping clean the home that is our house, the home that is our body, and the home that is our mind and psyche. Its gusts may be fierce and merciless, but profoundly clarifying. They liberate and release all that is stagnant, negative, and harmful, and make way for all that is vibrant, positive, and healthy.

This trecena is not the time for control or rules. It is a time of fluidity, experimentation, and open-mindedness. It's not a coincidence that the purer your mind and spirit and the healthier your body, the more clear and powerful your ability to communicate. Be one with the Wind, and experience a different kind of freedom!

Hun (1) Ik'
Jun (1) Iq'

Today is a day to purify, cleanse, clear out any negative, harmful or toxic elements, influences or forces in your life. Whatever it is—an illness, a chronic bad habit, a fear or phobia, a complaining or nagging friend or loved one, or a boss that keeps you down, you have the support today to start the process of flushing out the negative and bringing in the positive.

For those of you who've been thinking about this but haven't found the time or the motivation to do it, today is the day. Harness the strong kick-start energy of Hun and just do it!

Ka (2) Akb'al
Kieb (2) Aq'ab'al

It is at night when the greatest and most profound mysteries come to life, when your inner senses sharpen and awaken, and the promise of potential becomes real. Borne aloft fast and furious by the winds of Ik', Akb'al intensifies your powers of communication and clarification. So whatever you have to communicate or clarify today, trust in your inner night and do it! The energy of Ka will double the power of your words, already strengthened by Ik'.

Ox (3) Kan
Oxib' (3) K'at

Today's energy forecast, brought to you by Ox, calls for high winds, variable temperatures, and unstable pressure systems. Unless you're spiritually and psychologically well prepared, stay grounded and close to home today—whether that means physically, psychically, or both. This will give you a solid foundation from which you can safely deal with and deflect whatever challenges Ox throws at you today. Remember that although Ox can tangle Kan's finely woven net, Kan can in turn ensnare Ox's energies of uncertainty, doubt, and risk. So there is nothing pre-ordained; it all depends on your personal strength of character and will.

Kan (4) Chicchan
Kahib' (4) Cimi

The magical, powerful Serpent is a bit at odds with the Wind (it's Ik's trecena), which threatens to unravel and dissipate its energies. But Kan pulls them both in, grounding them in the four corners of the Earth and Sky.

Translation? Regardless of what goes on around you, whatever commotion or noise tries to distract or destabilize you, stay connected to your soul source, the mast of your ship, the path beneath your feet. Stay connected with your inner guide—only this way will you transcend the test of life's challenges.

Ho (5) Cimi
Job' (5) Kame

Eternity has no deadlines. Time neither begins nor ends; it simply flows and cycles. Yet we rush about, anxious how little time we have, competing to get ahead, to achieve certain things before our peers or neighbors do. If we can only remember that each one of us has his or her own individual time cycles of life, death and rebirth, of transformation, that we should not compare our lifepaths with those of anyone else. Slow down and spend some time with your personal innate rhythms, your natural timeline, and you'll move much faster toward the realization of your potential.

Be at complete peace with who you are.

Uac (6) Manik'
Wakib' (6) Kej

If you climb to the top of the mountain on your own two feet, you will feel the breath of the high winds with your own soul.

Today, Uac, the number of ultimate stability and wholeness, stands head to head with Manik', the nagual of the four corners of the Earth. No matter how high you climb, how far you fly, or how deep you dive, rely on Manik' and Uac to support you every step of the way. Trust their guidance and level-headed stability, but recognize the ultimate responsibility for your decisions and your actions, still lies in your hands, and your hands only.

Uuc (7) Lamat
Wukub' (7) Q'anil

The sign of Lamat reflects and magnifies the natural abundance we are all made of, vibrating at the higher frequencies of consciousness that generate the kind of exuberant, boundless vitality in mind, body and psyche that we all seek in one way or another. So relax and release the boundaries and limitations you impose on yourself. Just take care not to give others too much of yourself, or let Ik', the Wind, disperse your generosity too far and wide, lest you feel drained and exhausted.

Uaxac (8) Muluc
Wajxaqib' (8) Toj

When Water or Fire are lashed by the Wind, their effect and force intensifies exponentially. Were it not for Uaxac's stabilizing, grounding influence, there is no telling what kind of storm Muluc would whip up today. In fact, Uaxac empowers you to direct and harness the overwhelming power Muluc embodies—as Uaxac winds the cord of time around Muluc throughout the course of the day, you can funnel its energies toward the question, situation or goal you are working on or would like to address.

Bolon (9) Oc
B'elejeb' (9) Tz'i

An extremely positive and powerful day to cleanse your inner home—your soul, your heart, your body—of any vices, bad habits or negative thinking that have been holding you back or causing difficulty in your life. Carried by the strong winds of Ik' and blessed by the propitious energy of Bolon, Oc helps you dissolve and clear out the negative influences in your life that can be so tenacious and impede your soul's progress. Take advantage of this powerful day to free yourself from these burdens forever—or at the very least, start the process.

Lahun (10) Chuen
Lajuj (10) B'atz'

Today is a highly propitious day for an engagement or wedding. Lahun's close connection to family, society, and the relationship between two lovers intertwines with Chuen's powerful partnership essence, forging a marriage of energies that support and nourish your and your partner's soul. And for those of you already married, Lahun Chuen days are wonderful to renew your love and commitment to each other.

Buluk (11) Eb
Junlajuj (11) E'

The very act of traveling, of moving, of going somewhere clears the mind and frees the spirit. Motion is, in fact, the natural state of life itself—air molecules, light particles, water droplets, radio waves, the cells in our bodies, the thoughts we think and the emotions we feel, everything is constantly moving. The opposite, stasis or inaction, is death. So embrace the lifepath you are traveling, enjoy it, learn from it and marvel at it. But keep your focus consciously on your soul's horizon and your life's purpose, lest your lifepath veer off course.

La Ka (12) Ben
Kablajuj (12) Aj

It is always much easier to criticize or opine about others; yet when it comes to our own actions and words, suddenly everything seems a lot rosier and more forgiveable. Today, take into consideration the impact and influence your words or actions may have had on your family, whether on an individual loved one or collectively, and whether in the distant or recent past, or the present. If you accept the responsibility as yours, and communicate with your family sincerely and directly, you may be surprised how much peace and goodwill that creates.

Oxlahun (13) Ix
Oxlajuj (13) I'x

This is the day Ix the Jaguar manifests, emerging from the deep humid shadows of the jungle. Mirror your soul in his eyes, let go of your fears, feel deep inside you that archetypal power to know all living things and bring dreams forth into reality... before the Jaguar slips into the dark green depths again.

And so we come to a deep and velvety close of Ik's trecena, holding close within the personal and intimate insights we've learned—and will hopefully hold for a long time to come. That's the key to the trecenas of the Tzolk'in... embody the knowledge you attain.

Men / Tz'ikin
Ruler of the Trecena of Vision

original artwork, printed here in black & white,
courtesy of Maree Gifkins

MEN / TZ'IKIN
The Trecena of Vision

Men, or Tz'ikin in K'iche' Maya, is the far-seeing Eagle, the great bird that soars far above the highest peaks of mountains and pyramids, high above the din of mankind, where only sacred silence and the breath of winds reign. Sweeping across vast stretches of sky on broad powerful wings, Men enters the dreams of men and women to impart important messages and revelations. Made of legend, his breadth and acuity of vision surpasses that of any other living thing, and that is why this day sign embodies vision, clarity, perception, and profound understanding. Men is the Guardian of the Sun and cosmic space, and the eloquent mediator between the opposing viewpoints of *Uk'ux Kaj* and *Uk'ux Ulew* (Heart of Sky, Heart of Earth). As the nagual of good fortune and economic well-being, Men embodies wealth, financial health and business affairs and negotiations. Men's animal totems are the eagle and *maq'uq'*, the sacred quetzal bird. In the Classical Maya tradition, it is associated with the cardinal direction West and the color black. In the tradition of modern-day K'iche' Maya, it is East and the color red.

On Men days, the Maya give their thanks and gratitude for whatever prosperity and material well-being they enjoy, and sincerely express the intention that more may come into their lives. Men is, in fact, the day to dedicate the *Xukulem Chuwach Ri Qajaw*, a sacred Mayan ceremony to ask for good luck. It is also the best day in the Tzolk'in for love, friendship, and abundance, for each person as well as for the community. We may also ask for protection for our businesses.

Come along for a 36,000-foot view of your life as you soar far above the routine, the day-to-day that keeps you from seeing your golden horizon and connecting with your destiny. Men the Eagle will sweep you off your feet and show you the path your life is carving through time, so that you may see where it's going and decide how to guide its future progress. Only Tz'ikin can give you this view—the very name of this day sign derives from *Tz'i*, the sign of Authority we have already read about, and the Maya word for the Sun, *k'in*.

In our fast-paced, stressed society where being busy and having a top flight career is prized far above health and family, where success is defined by material wealth and personal status, there is little room for what truly matters. Modern society is built upon control and influence—the media, the economy, the political system, organized religion, even the workplace and our own families can be extremely limiting. But we can change that. We can re-arrange our schedules, redefine and re-establish our priorities, and insist on them for every aspect of our lives. Each one of us really does have a choice, regardless of what our bosses, colleagues, peers—and yes, even our own families—may say. The only things keeping us from making the choices we want to make, at the end of the day, are fear, uncertainty, and the force of habit. This is what Men helps us clear away, by taking us far out and above the grinding tasks and mental patterns that rule our daily lives.

Unfetter the shackles of belief, fear, and uncertainty that hold you down. Break down the walls of what others tell you. This is a time for you to explore who you really are: your higher self, your dreams and ambitions, your ultimate potential.

Careful, though, not to act too quickly or impulsively, for these soaring heights can be intoxicating. When you witness pure potential, when you feel the exhilaration of freedom, it's like a drug. The air is purer, you can see farther, you can fly faster and stronger. But this trecena is about vision, not action. So take these thirteen days to clear your sight and your perspective, work through where you want your life's path to take you, or where it is already taking you, and prepare to take action in due time.

Remember, flight at these heights takes experience, planning, and skill. So take your time to learn to navigate the great Eagle's wings, and don't forget to enjoy the view.

Hun (1) Men
Jun (1) Tz'ikin

If you have ever dreamed of starting something big, something momentous and breathtaking, do it today. Men and Hun will take you high up above the doubting, disbelieving thomases that have been holding you back—including yourself!—and launch you on your first solo flight into a new world, a world that may leave you breathless and intoxicated, but certainly never wanting to look back. But just as you wouldn't leap from a cliff with no wings or parachute, make the right preparations for your own personal and unique quantum jump.

Ka (2) Cib
Kieb (2) Ajmaq

Today enables you to get insight and clarity on something from your past, perhaps from your ancestral line, that has been on your mind or that has been bothering you and you have not been able to figure things out using traditional means.

Careful not to overanalyze, or overreact to, your insights however! The duality of Ka (Two) is quite powerful and will give you a multitude of perspectives from all sides of a given issue, but it can also render you rather indecisive if you don't hold steady.

Ox (3) Caban
Oxib' (3) No'j

Another challenging Caban day, made all the more so by the energy of Three, which represents risk, uncertainty, doubt and obstruction. Steer clear of trying to complete personal projects, making plans or starting anything new, whether a relationship, buying a house, or planning social engagements.

The best use of today may be to flex your mental muscle and practice letting go of negative thinking and negative thoughts—let them come, recognize them, but deny them power. Then let them go.

Kan (4) Etznab
Kahib' (4) Tijax

Like a gleaming new machete in the thick darkness of the jungle, wield Etznab's energy to cut through to the core truth of things, peeling away layers of deception, half-truths, misplaced perceptions so that you can be whole again. Shed the ego and its complexities like an old skin you no longer need, and stretch those wings— remember this is a Men trecena—to carry you to a purer, simpler, higher ground.

Ho (5) Cauac
Job' (5) Kawoq

If you could get early warnings about any health issues about to break, would you act on them? And if you could prevent health problems altogether, would you do what's necessary? If your answer is yes on both counts, then today is the day to start. Cauac, a highly auspicious day for health, healing and overall well-being, joins Ho, carrying emerging ahead-of-their-time energies, to give you the head-start you need to fortify and protect your health, one of the most neglected areas of our lives. But don't delay. No matter how great you feel, make this commitment to yourself today and renew it each Ho Cauac day.

Uac (6) Ahau
Wakib' (6) Ajpu

Never were a warrior and his weapon better matched: Uac is the golden lance in Ahau's arsenal. Embodying ultimate stability and a steadfastly practical approach to life's challenges, Uac lays the solid ground you'll need to stand on to resolve your toughest trials, your greatest struggles, while Ahau, Lord of the Sun, burns a clear path into that ground for you with an intensity of insight and intuition that can only originate from the highest of vantage points.

As Men the Eagle, the ruler of this trecena, soars over the lifepath of your soul, turn your face into the sun and recharge your mind, body and spirit.

Uuc (7) Imix
Wukub' (7) Imox

Careful out there today... wound around otherworldly Imix, the spintop energy of Uuc (Seven) will have you flying from one state of reality to another, running multiple trains of thought on the same track; if you let it all spin out of control, you can easily lose yourself. So pace yourself, and listen to what Imix is really telling you.

Uuc also represents endings, which could put an end to a state of mind, a relationship, or an entire way of life—and inspire another. Rather than fear the end—of whatever it may be—accept and embrace it as a natural part of life and of consciousness.

Uaxac (8) Ik'
Wajxaqib' (8) Iq'

If a situation in your life calls for diplomacy, today is the day for it. Uaxac helps you see and understand things from a holistic perspective, while Ik', the energy of connectedness and communication, held aloft by Men's outstretched wings, enables clarity of vision and concise, concrete expression. Your job is to navigate the situation at hand with an even, neutral keel, avoiding personal agendas, egos or manipulative tendencies, be they within you, apparent in others, or both.

Bolon (9) Akb'al
B'elejeb' (9) Aq'ab'al

If you are engaged, try to set your wedding date for today, Nine Akb'al, for Akb'al is a most propitious day for love, romance and marriage, and Nine was the most favored day by the ancient Maya for important ceremonies. You may also propose to your partner, announce your engagement, or celebrate your anniversary on this day. And if you don't have any planned events or ceremonies, don't feel you've missed out—it's a great day to tell the man or woman you love, that you do.

Lahun (10) Kan
Lajuj (10) K'at

If there is anything or anyone exercising negative influence on you or your life, or holding you back in any way, especially if these influences are rooted in the past, today is a good day to neutralize that impact, resolve whatever hidden causes may be driving it, and make a clean break from the toxic influence—or at least start the process. And to help you, rely on Lahun's innate resonance with human relationships and cooperation, so that you may call on those around you who love and support you. Don't go it alone if you don't have to.

Buluk (11) Chicchan
Junlajuj (11) Kan

You hold a deep, ancient power within you, within your body and soul that modern society has all but forgotten... and that those who rule our world don't want you to remember. This is the power to evolve to the highest levels of your potential—but you must first shed the old skins of fear, anxiety, and lack of self-love and self-respect. Shed these skins like the Serpent sheds its winter scales, ignite anew your true *koyopa*, and soar refreshed and revitalized from the ashes of your previously unfulfilled self to heights as yet unimagined.

La Ka (12) Cimi
Kablajuj (12) Kame

The experience of life can be agony and it can be ecstasy; it can be effortless and it can be impossibly difficult; it can bring pain as easily as it brings joy. These are not opposing sides, nor do they conflict— they are merely different expressions of one face. You must feel and experience them all to understand what it means to live, so that you may die to live again in a future lifetime. This is the wisdom of the ancestors, the soul elders who guide us from beyond and with whom Cimi connects us today.

Oxlahun (13) Manik'
Oxlajuj (13) Kej

The greatest power is always invisible. It's the songs in your heart, the thoughts in your mind, the images you dream for your life. Who wrote those songs, who put those thoughts in your head, who painted those dreams? If they are not yours, someone has stolen your power away.

Take it back. Take back the power that is innately yours, yours at birth and yours at death. Weave a sacred *koyopa* cord with Oxlahun's energy and place it around the neck of Manik', the great stag—and ride forth to retrieve the soul power that has always been yours!

Lamat / Q'anil
Ruler of the Trecena of Abundance

*original artwork, printed here in black & white,
courtesy of Maree Gifkins*

LAMAT / Q'ANIL
The Trecena of Abundance

Alush and fertile sign, Lamat, or Q'anil in K'iche' Maya, brims with the energy of positive growth and abundance. Lamat carries the codes for all of life, nourishes perpetual regeneration, and represents the seed, corn, pride, harvest, and food. A harmonious and cyclical day, it also symbolizes love, understanding, and realization, and embodies ancestral knowledge, universal memory and genetic wisdom. Lamat is the nagual of all kinds of animal and plant seeds, and the day sign of fertility and harvests, of prosperity and abundance. It signifies corn and its four colors known to the Maya: yellow, white, red and black—which are also the four colors of the twenty day signs in the Tzolk'in, represented by the four cardinal directions of the globe. In fact, the four colors and directions are represented by the four points within the glyph itself. The animal totem of Lamat is the rabbit. In the Classical Maya tradition, it is associated with the cardinal direction South and the color yellow. In the tradition of modern-day K'iche' Maya, it is West and the color black.

On Lamat days, the Maya plant ideas and new projects along with gardens and crops, for this is the day that all things are made fertile and blossom. Anything planted or conceived on a Lamat day, whether it is an idea, project, relationship or an actual seed, holds a positive future and is likely to bear fruit or turn out favorably, all in due time. This is also a propitious day to recover something presumed to be lost.

Take these next 13 days to enjoy and celebrate the abundance in your life, without guilt, without hesitation: celebrate who you are, what you bring to this world and your loved ones, and what your loved ones and the world around you, in turn bring to you. Let us remember what true abundance really is: it's not money or fame, and it's not power or influence. Abundance is life in its breathtaking diversity of forms and colors. Abundance is the unfathomable volumes of sunlight, water, air and nutrients that cycle throughout the biosphere. Abundance is a rich harvest that leaves plenty of fruits, vegetables, and grain for the next season or to share with your neighbors. Abundance is an endlessly overflowing fountain of joy, elation, and happiness that never dries up and never asks for anything in return. Abundance is that nobility of spirit that keeps no score and no grudges, a spirit completely content and free of toxic emotions and thoughts.

Abundance is the natural state of the planet—and humanity.

But we, human beings, tend to be so wrapped up in our careers, our to-do lists, our responsibilities and productivity goals, that we miss all of this wondrous abundance flowing around and through us on a continual, daily basis. We willingly drown our spirit in fears, worries, and uncertainties, allowing these forces to take over our lives and our very existence, drop by drop, day by day, until we are positively frightened to feel good about anything.

This is dangerous. By denying the natural abundance inherent in our lives, we are stunting our own spiritual growth, our mental and physical health, the wellbeing of our families and loved ones—and yes, ironically, our financial health as well. Remember that linear upward trends are not natural or healthy, contrary to what the media, political figures, and economic pundits would have you believe. Cycles, waves and the duality of upward and downward trends are natural and necessary in all aspects of life to maintain sustained abundance. Our culture assigns moral values to these natural cycles—up is "good" and down is "bad"—which then motivate certain behaviors and drive certain actions in our lives, relationships, social and political spheres, and the economy, that run contrary to the creation of lasting abundance, wealth, and prosperity. By worshipping greed, short-term profits, and material riches, we sacrifice the sanctity of a far greater source of abundance—our own nature and essence.

Think about what living an abundant, joyous, fulfilling life really means to you, and pursue that—not the plastic ideals of modern life you see and hear in the media and on the Internet. Do not allow the poison of envy, greed, inferiority or inequality to enter the vessels of your soul. Respect your natural merit and worthiness of a full and enriching life.

This trecena, *choose* to live in breathtaking abundance.

Hun (1) Lamat
Jun (1) Q'anil

Of particular importance is this trecena's first day, Hun (One) Lamat, as the strong initiating energy of Hun duplicates Lamat's power to multiply all things to abundance. Whatever it is you wish to enhance and drive to abundance in your life, whether it's emotional, spiritual, physical or material, and whoever it's for, whether it's you or a loved one, engage Lamat and Hun, and do it today.

Enjoy who you are, truly, fully and completely, without guilt or comparisons against others—for only then can you multiply your potential and your joy to the levels of abundance that you desire.

Ka (2) Muluc
Kieb (2) Toj

To achieve true equilibrium, you need to walk the golden line that lies precisely in the middle of any two extremes. The concept is simple, but its practice is anything but. There is always a light side to the dark, a yin polarity to the yang, a right for every wrong. Our challenge in life is to balance the charges, especially those we carry into this lifetime with our personal karma, and do so without ego, judgment, or desire for vengeance. Only then can we enter a state of grace, peace, and abundance. Use Muluc's and Ka's balancing energies to harmonize your life and reconcile whatever karmic debts are still pending.

Ox (3) Oc
Oxib' (3) Tz'i

The energy of Ox calls into question anything you do today that involves your personal authority, the law, or your quest for justice, in whatever sense of the word. So no matter how sure you are of yourself, steer clear of legal matters, and do not seek to use your authority in ways that influence or impact others. Do not start anything new or make major changes to any aspect of your life. Instead, focus on identifying, isolating and releasing any bad habits, negative thinking or personal vices, and making energetic space for abundance and prosperity.

Kan (4) Chuen
Kahib' (4) B'atz'

Just as Nature and the Universe have their sacred geometries, so too do we, human beings. The human body is one of the most extraordinary models of natural design and engineering, and the human mind is one of the most intricate and complex embodiments of living consciousness. Respect and honor your body and mind—the food you eat, the thoughts you think, the forms of exercise you choose, the rest you grant yourself, the people you welcome into your inner life, are all critical balancing elements you need to live in complete harmony. And so, if your mind and body are natural works of art, you are the artist. Honor the artist of your soul.

Ho (5) Eb
Job' (5) E'

Many of us are taught to think we have one path in life we call "destiny." In fact, we walk many paths throughout our lives, paths that may vary greatly in length, beauty, difficulty and lessons learned. These are the paths that make up the greater road our souls travel as we fulfill our purpose in this lifetime. That is what makes our human experience so poignant and so rich. Celebrate the abundance of paths in your life, whether past, present or future, and embrace them all fully, completely and wholeheartedly.

Uac (6) Ben
Wakib' (6) Aj

One of the most wholesome and abundant days in the Tzolk'in. Ben settles into the nourishing embrace of Lamat, and together they are enveloped by the solid, stable energy of Uac (Six). The resulting energy is orders of magnitude more abundant, more wholesome, more complete than either of the three on their own.

Ground your spirit well within your internal home, the essence of your soul. From here, from this single elemental source, all aspects of your life can be healed, made whole, and fresh and vibrant again.

Uuc (7) Ix
Wukub' (7) I'x

The law of the jungle is ruthless. Some must die so that others may live. Unforgiving competition for resources, perpetual struggle to ensure survival of your own species. Yet there is also breathtaking beauty, harmony and balance, and a spectacular abundance of sunlight, water and nutrients for all to partake. It all depends on how you look at life... Uuc helps you see things from all sides, and Ix guides you to attain your goals according to your own innate, natural purpose, intention and talents.

As in the jungle, so in life.

Uaxac (8) Men
Wajxaqib' (8) Tz'ikin

A great day to give thanks for the well-being, wealth and abundance in your life, and to ask for more without any guilt or timidity. Despite Western values of humility and frugality, ours is a society that worships wanton consumption and materialism that exceed the bounds of sustainable prosperity. Native people like the Maya, on the other hand, have no issue with wealth. For them, prosperity is a perfectly acceptable and desirable part of life. But they know how to balance their needs and desires with what the Earth and their communities can provide.

Bolon (9) Cib
B'elejeb' (9) Ajmaq

There are certain sacred energies that have no boundaries, no limits and no restrictions. Forgiveness is one of them. In the context of the trecena of Lamat, Cib pulses with an abundance of forgiveness and understanding. When you seek pardon or a release from guilt arising from any wrongdoing on your part, remember you need to forgive yourself first. Bolon's presence assures a positive response from your ancestors and the ancient energies that are present in your life.

Lahun (10) Caban
Lajuj (10) No'j

Buoyed by the nourishing energy of Lamat and the warm, human bonds symbolized by Lahun (Ten), today Caban encourages us to enjoy the company of our friends and loved ones, even as we contemplate those relationships in all of their diversity and richness. And the less ego and emotion we color our thoughts with, the more love we infuse into our perception, the deeper comprehension and clarity we will attain.

Buluk (11) Etznab
Junlajuj (11) Tijax

Call things by their name. Don't console yourself with fantasies, self-deception or wishful thinking, no matter how tempting it is. Painful as it may be at any given moment, the truth is the only thing that can ever set you free. Unrealistic ideals, denial and escape may appear to buy you time in the short run, but in reality they steal it, for they set you back and deny you the time you need to build your dreams into reality. Buluk intensifies Etznab's energy by several orders of magnitude—and because it's a neutral force, it may not give you the rosy picture you were hoping for. Be strong! Sometimes the raw truth is what you need to move forward in life.

La Ka (12) Cauac
Kablajuj (12) Kawoq

Reflect on the path and experience of your life so far, in peace and tranquility. Do not judge, simply reflect and consider, so that you may discern how best to adjust your lifepath to direct it toward your most desired horizon. Today, you can choose the quality of the Rainstorm you want or need: a hard, driving cyclone to wash away lingering negative thoughts, habits, or patterns; a soft, nurturing rain to grow new seeds you have planted; or perhaps a sensual, tropical storm to stir up your creative juices. Cauac's energy has infinite power and infinite possibility—use it fully and use it well.

Oxlahun (13) Ahau
Oxlajuj (13) Ajpu

Be patient with, do not judge or disparage, those who can't seem to keep up with you or your progress—but at the same time try to rise ever higher and faster to face and conquer your own most extreme challenges. Lit up by the vibrant energy of Ahau, the nagual of the Sun, Oxlahun spirals into a tightly wound coil of sacred psychic energy, springloading a quantum jump to the completion of all processes, journeys and experiences that you have been moving through recently. Reflect with your heart, mind and body on what you have learned so that you may apply it on a higher level in the next cycle.

IMIX / IMOX
RULER OF THE TRECENA OF INSPIRATION

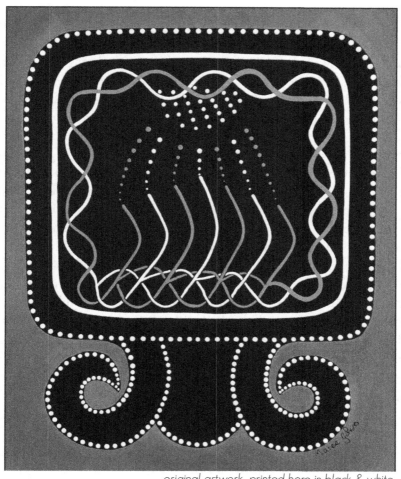

*original artwork, printed here in black & white,
courtesy of Maree Gifkins*

IMIX / IMOX
The Trecena of Inspiration

Associated with powerful psychic forces, Imix, or Imox in K'iche' Maya, represents what is often called the "left side of reality"—those other dimensions, worlds, levels of existence that are unusual, eccentric, or in general deemed outside of what is "normal." Accordingly, Imix symbolizes not only the receptivity to communication with or messages from these other realities and the ability to see into other worlds, but also madness, insanity, mental disorder, nervousness, uncertainty, and doubt. Imix is a difficult day sign, for these things are not simple to navigate or understand; in fact, they can be altogether frightening. Yet Imix also signifies cooperation, especially in terms of the left arm working in concert with the right. Stupidity, envy, suspicion, and secretiveness round out the pantheon of traits and elements embodied by this complex day sign. Imix is the nagual of the ocean and the spirit of rain, and has a powerful connection with water. Not surprisingly, the animal totems of Imix are the dolphins, whales, fish, crocodiles, and all sea creatures. In the Classical Maya tradition, it is associated with the cardinal direction East and the color red. In the tradition of modern-day K'iche' Maya, it is North and the color white.

On Imix days, the Maya give thanks, ask for rain and water, and pray that their dreams and visions bring them beauty and wisdom rather than delusions and madness. This is the day to pay attention to our dreams and the wisdom they may bring, to heal and cure illnesses of the mind, and to pray for strong mental health, not just for us but also for our loved ones. And it is, as Imix is closely connected with water, a highly beneficial day to spend near a stream, river or the ocean.

There is a very fine line between inspiration and madness. How do you know whether an idea or vision that comes to you is the next great novel or ground-breaking technology, or simply a crazy idea? Who decides what is normal and what is strange? Why is it that for native cultures such as the Maya, smoking hallucinogenic plants is part of a sacred rite that only specially trained members of their communities, namely the shamans, can undergo, while in modern Western society, smoking or taking drugs—also derived from plants—is usually a way to disconnect, have fun, or escape the stresses of daily life and carries no sacred values or associated rituals? Is one wrong and the other right?

Everything that we do and think, every aspect of our personal and family life, culture, politics, profession, nationality, race, and religion, is relative. It all depends on how we handle situations, people, and concepts that are foreign or different from what we're used to. Some of us welcome the strange, the unusual, the new; some of us prefer the comfort of predictability and familiarity even if it's not always the best thing for us and our personal development.

If you're an artist, traveler, entrepreneur, or a creative type in general, you are likely capable of handling Imix's volatile energies with greater ease and ability than most. As its mutable essence percolates through this next trecena, focus on strengthening your creative spirit and the power of your mind, and dive into the vast ocean of ideas, concepts, dreams, and possibilities that Imix blasts open. Be aware there is no instruction manual or safety rope here, so don't overestimate your ability to navigate the conflicting realities mixing around you. Keep your humility and respect for this day sign, and you will emerge with a stronger, brighter, richer mind.

If you favor predictability, constancy, and familiarity, better stay home and keep the wild forces of Imix at bay. You might in fact prefer to watch the daring artist types go in head first, from the warm comfort of your couch! In fact, the Maya themselves avoid any appreciable amount of activity, because for them, Imix is a challenging day, charged with reflecting the deep, visionary aspect of reality... not unlike, as author Ken Johnson describes it, Carl Jung's concept of the collective unconscious.

Whatever your personal character, take this time to explore and test the boundaries of your own reality, however vast or limited they may be. Just be sure you have a rock-solid core to keep you steady and strong.

Hun (1) Imix
Jun (1) Imox

Where is an idea truly born? Does it germinate within the mind, outside the mind, or perhaps in another dimension? That is one of the great mysteries of human consciousness, and a very appropriate one to ponder today. Hun is the seed of all thoughts, the stem cell of all ideas, the DNA of inspiration. But when these seeds are planted in Imix soil, they don't all bloom fragrant flowers. So take care where and what you sow today: it is your intention that determines how your ideas and thoughts will manifest tomorrow.

Ka (2) Ik'
Kieb (2) Iq'

A time to dream, a time to act; a time to plan, a time to execute. Let Ik' power your intentions into material reality, but grab firm hold of the wild Wind's reins, lest its awesome force overtake you and divert your efforts into a different reality than the one you intended. Whatever you have started now, in this trecena, thunders toward completion, so stay focused and on your path. Do not let your sails fold under the power of the Wind—use it instead to propel your intentions forward.

Ox (3) Akb'al
Oxib' (3) Aq'ab'al

Beware of the other face of Night: the unknown, unseen and unheard can be terrifying, especially when your own perceptions play tricks on your mind. Ox's precarious energy infuses this day with uncertainty which can quickly turn to fear—for the seed of potential knows no emotion or value. It simply is. To make matters worse, we are in the trecena of Imix, which pulls in alternate realities and the potential for going a bit mad. Perhaps better to stay at home mentally today.

Kan (4) Kan
Kahib' (4) Ka't

Kan can be a rather volatile day sign, and needs numbers like its namesake, Kan (Four) to ground its passions in tranquility and wholeness. Together, Kan and Kan can travel to the four corners of the world and achieve great things. Harness that energy today for the good of your own dreams and aspirations: whatever aspect of Kan the day sign you choose to work with, whether it's liberating yourself from oppressive habits, situations or relationships, enhancing your physical, artistic or spiritual fertility, or casting your net farther and wider to bring in the resources you need, guide your actions with the wholesome, stabilizing energy of Kan the number.

Ho (5) Chicchan
Job' (5) Kan

One of Chicchan's lesser known traits is that it is the nagual of education and training. If you want to get ahead in life, one of the best and surest ways to get there, is to do what you do extremely well. And that means knowledge, education, and practical experience. So don't delay any longer—take that course or seminar, apply for that degree, attend that mixer or conference! Whatever your goal—be it learning a new language or deepening a specific personal talent or activity you're passionate about—Chicchan supports your education and training, and Ho pushes you to get ahead as early on in your journey as possible.

Uac (6) Cimi
Wakib' (6) Kame

Whatever is causing pain or sorrow, whatever is blocking you or your progress—whether it's your thoughts, people or events—Cimi holds powerful energy to help you work through the blockages and the obstacles in your inner and outer life. But don't leave home without Uac's level-headed, practical approach, for if you rely on Cimi alone in this trecena (it's Imix!), you might end up on the other side of reality. Keep a steady, pragmatic mindset, and the right solutions will present themselves at the right time.

Uuc (7) Manik'
Wukub' (7) Kej

In life, sooner or later you have to choose sides, make a decision, voice an opinion. Uuc may make that difficult today for the mighty Manik'; but instead of teetering on the edge of indecision or avoiding taking a stand, turn the tables and use the neutrality of Uuc to see straight through agendas, intrigues, deceptions and maneuvres. Direct Manik's power toward truth, integrity, honor, and respect, and you shall stand in awe at the mountains you move.

Uaxac (8) Lamat
Wajxaqib' (8) Q'anil

True abundance and prosperity should be effortless. Natural. We are taught to believe that it can only be achieved through hard work, and indeed most of our societal systems, customs, and practices in place today would make it so. Yet all babies are born with an overflowing abundance of spirit, mind and body—this is the natural source of vitality that gets drained over time. Take the time today to relax, rest and rejuvenate your thoughts, your psyche and your body. Start taking back the natural, inherent abundance and joy that was yours at birth.

Bolon (9) Muluc
B'elejeb' (9) Toj

Today, all is fluid, flowing, shifting, changing... giving you new and unique perspectives and insights into whatever it is you are dealing with at the moment. No matter how tough or impossible a situation may seem, take hope, for Bolon carries extremely positive, nourishing energies, and Muluc embodies the balance, harmony, and inner peace you need to overcome your greatest challenges. Rather than expecting or hoping for life's struggles to stop, stay balanced and flexible, and acknowledge your karmic debt with humility so that you may easily work through anything that comes across your life's path.

Lahun (10) Oc
Lajuj (10) Tz'i

Your personal authority can make a big difference today in bringing people together for a common purpose or in improving relationships, whether yours or those of others. Stay mentally and emotionally balanced as you connect with your loved ones to resolve any silent issues that have gone undiscussed or unaddressed and are still causing friction or misunderstanding. If you have spiritual authority in your community, use it to forge or reaffirm strong bonds among members, but do not abuse it to serve your own agenda or boost your personal status or power.

Buluk (11) Chuen
Junlajuj (11) B'atz'

What happens when you dunk Chuen the Monkey into the psychedelics of Imix? Your ocean turns into a mountain, time ties itself into an infinite bow, and your thoughts flow backwards. It's the perfect day to tear down all limitations and boundaries, and explore completely new and unheard-of ideas and concepts. Whatever you come up with, Buluk will only intensify it, as it's not only frightfully powerful, it's also a perfectly balanced, neutral number that makes no value judgment. That task is up to you.

La Ka (12) Eb
Kablajuj (12) E'

Eb, the bearer of time and conductor of destiny, leads us on the path toward our own La Ka horizon, representing the totality of our life experiences and influences, be they cultural, societal, familial or individual. Don't wait for the end of your journey to see, acknowledge and understand these influences; your life shall be made instantly richer, deeper, stronger, if you take a moment today to honor them now, in the present moment.

Oxlahun (13) Ben
Oxlajuj (13) Aj

Allow the sacred energy of Oxlahun to enter through your 13 major joints and merge with your own *koyopa* essence, giving you acutely enhanced intuition and perception. On this Ben day, use this power to stabilize and purify your inner soul, the home of your homes. If you can, share the experience with your loved ones, so that they too may benefit from today's energies. For it is only through true inner peace that the external places we call home can be filled with love, joy and contentment.

Ix / I'x
RULER OF THE TRECENA OF SOURCE

*original artwork, printed here in black & white,
courtesy of Maree Gifkins*

IX / I'X
The Trecena of Source

Mystical, magical, and close to Mother Earth, Ix, or I'x in K'iche' Maya, embodies the very soul of Nature and the spirit, energy, force, and vitality of life and all living things. The nagual of Nature and Mayan altars, it symbolizes the sacred energy pulsing through running water such as streams and brooks, and the protective energy of places like plains, hills, and mountains. Feline and feminine in nature, Ix represents innate intuition, curiosity, and the creative forces of the universe; in fact, this is the day sign that grants the spiritual and psychological strength to reach the highest levels of consciousness, which underpins mysticism and divination. It also rules the seven human sins—from the Maya point of view: pride, ambition, envy, lies, crime, ingratitude, and ignorance through laziness. The animal totem of Ix is the jaguar. In the Classical Maya tradition, it is associated with the cardinal direction North and the color white. In the tradition of modern-day K'iche' Maya, it is South and the color yellow.

Ix days are days of high magic and divination. The Maya set aside a household altar or a special space in the home for prayer and meditation, with incense, candles and other suitable items. This is the day to spend in meditation and introspection so that we may contemplate our lifepath and redirect it as needed or desired. Ix days help attain mental and physical fortitude. Given its feminine nature, on an Ix day we should also honor the work of women.

The Jaguar is one of the most enigmatic and mystical animals on earth. In Maya lore, Ix is an *Ajpop*, a higher deity, of the American jungles. Called *mano de lana* in South America ("the woolen hand") for its soundless, soft step that you don't hear until it's too late, the Jaguar embodies the very source of Mother Earth. Its deep, feminine energy heals as well as culls, bearing a profound intuition about the essence of all things. It fuses power with strategic insight, patiently retracing the footsteps of time until that critical split-second of decisive action. Endowed with extraordinary strength and resilience, Ix carries intelligence often paired with clairvoyance—no surprise, as this powerful day sign is free of the debilitating effects of ego, ambition, judgment, fear, and control.

When you connect to your source, remember that this too is your own soul—this primal, unspoken, ancient energy that underpins our individual and collective consciousness. Here, no ego, no judgment, no self-doubt or fear exist, for these mindsets are far too close to the surface of our human emotions to have any impact on the ancient archetypes, the elemental currents underlying life itself. Just as the deep ocean breathes unperturbed by the commotions at the water's surface high above, so the ancient energies of Ix cycle deep and strong through generation after generation regardless of the petty skirmishes that take up so much of our time.

Industrialized society keeps us all at the thin surface of our potential. The communication and messages carried by the media, in the workplace, at home, at social events, almost wherever you go today, continually pull you out to the external world, telling you that you should look a certain way, have a certain status, live a certain type of lifestyle. It keeps you entertained so you don't think, overfed so you don't move, scared so you don't risk. The non stop stream of media and commerce gushing at you from an ever-increasing number of channels and platforms, wants your attention 24x7. Today, you have to work at it if you want a bit of time and room for silence, for thoughtful reflection and meditation.

Ix brings you back in, into the depths of your soul, the vast ocean of personal power and potential beneath that thin surface where reality is much richer and more rewarding than anything the external world can give you. This doesn't mean you should leave the world you live in, or shun society—it simply opens the path to your deeper self. You can live and enjoy your full and complete soul and being right in the midst of the modern world—all you need is Ix's guidance.

Whether or not this is your birthsign, take the time to spend time with Ix this trecena, and all Ix days. Liberate yourself from the shackles of societal imprints, and walk the path of the Jaguar—alone, in tune with your own natural power.

Hun (1) Ix
Jun (1) I'x

Today begins the trecena of Ix, the enigmatic, mystical Jaguar. Like that first silken footstep that lands silent upon the jungle floor, like that first purring breath that reverberates among the trees before dawn, envelop your soul in the warm presence of the jaguar within, of Ix, the nagual of Nature and the spirit, and feel its sacred raw energy pulsate through your entire being.

Connect to your source and honor the deep, ancient energy of the collective soul that connects us all.

Ka (2) Men
Kieb (2) Tz'ikin

Soar high but stay grounded; let your ambitions fly unbounded but harness their energy with focus; gaze deep into the soul of things but understand their physical reality. These are the messages that spin off the union of Ka and Men today, as Ka highlights the inherent duality that's built into our existence and universal natural laws, and Men, the great mediator, helps us understand how to address opposing or disparate perspectives.

Ox (3) Cib
Oxib' (3) Ajmaq

You may feel a great deal of nervousness and uncertainty today as Cib pulls ancient lines of soul energy to your consciousness, lines that you may vaguely sense or simply not understand. It is important to know that this is the influence of Ox (Three), and not messages or instructions from your ancestors. To cut through the white noise, tune in with focus and attention but not judgment—any negative or unbalancing tendencies or thoughts that you sense, let them pass through and resolve on their own.

Kan (4) Caban
Kahib' (4) No'j

If you seek spiritual guidance, today is one of the best days to do so. The Maya consult their diviners on Caban days; but today Caban is further enhanced and complemented by the strong, stable energy of Four and the powerful, profound undercurrent of Ix, the ruler of this trecena. Open your heart and quiet your mind, and you will feel the sure, steady power of this blend of energies. Accept them as they are, without doubt, fear or opposition, and they will carry you ever closer to the horizon of your soul path.

It may feel almost effortless to seek guidance today; and that is the way it should be!

Ho (5) Etznab
Job' (5) Tijax

What would you do if you could prevent a disease, avoid a quarrel, or avert an accident? Today's energies, Ho and Etznab, give you the power to do just that: Ho brings you into a situation ahead of time, enabling the gift of foresight, while Etznab helps you cut through negative energies of all kinds. But you have to know how to harness and handle them both. If you don't know what you're doing, you may stumble into things too early or too unprepared, or use the wrong side of Etznab's blade.

Uac (6) Cauac
Wakib' (6) Kawoq

Are you up for the challenge of healing yourself completely, inside and out? If so, this is your day! Cauac carries powerful energies for health and well-being, while Uac brings in stability and a practical, pragmatic approach to life. When it comes to your health, nothing works like action steeped in concrete reality. So make the commitment today to your total well-being, from knowledge and awareness to practice and lifestyle: learn the facts about the impact of stress and excessive travel, choose an organic, plant-based diet, set up an exercise program that works for you, make time for rest and sleep, and modify your lifestyle to make your health a priority.

Uuc (7) Ahau
Wukub' (7) Ajpu

In a struggle, fight, or any kind of challenge or conflict, often you do not have the luxury of time to ponder the best next step. Uuc complicates this significantly by opening up all possible angles and points of view. You will need to focus on the ultimate goal you are striving to attain, and choose the right path to navigate through the challenges facing you to get there. Be strong and have courage, for you have powerful energies as your partners today: this is an Ahau day, and the trecena of Ix, the mighty Jaguar.

Uaxac (8) Imix
Wajxaqib' (8) Imox

If you're going through a stressful time, no matter how maddening it feels, no matter how desperately you want to escape the situation, trust in the guidance of Uaxac. As it threads the cord of time through the psychic fabric that Imix weaves at each iteration of its passing in the cycle of the Tzolk'in, it will show you the way out of the dark jungles of life into the light you seek. Follow Uaxac's cord, never letting go, and you will make it through.

Bolon (9) Ik'
B'elejeb' (9) Iq'

The Wind blows not from the North or South, East or West, but from within you. Seek the core source of your soul and guide it to the place it needs to be, upon the path you seek. Let Bolon rain its golden essence and propitious energies all over Ik's powerful winds, saturating them to the extreme. Release them deep, far and wide throughout all aspects of your life so that they may sweep it clean of dust and stagnation and infuse it with joy and elation.

Lahun (10) Akb'al
Lajuj (10) Aq'ab'al

Devote time and attention to your marriage or love relationhip today. Forge stronger bonds of friendship, partnership, and collaboration, for it is your partner who will be there for you for the rest of your life—if that is what you both desire. Don't take your partner for granted; honor him or her with love, compassion and understanding, give him or her the freedom to be who they are, without reservation or judgment. Do not ask for money or material wealth, but build it together. Know yourselves, share your dreams and live in integrity and peace.

Buluk (11) Kan
Junlajuj (11) K'at

Revere and respect your fertile soul, for deep in you—whether you're woman or man—lies the sacred capacity to create life and breathe it into your intentions, whatever form it may ultimately take. Creativity and fertility are vital forces that constantly cycle through opposing yet complementary, ever-perpetuating rhythms—like the rise and descent of the Sun, the inhale and exhale of your every breath, the ebb and flow of air and water—that ignite the spark of existence within ideas, concepts, and nascent living things.

There is no higher power than that which creates life.

La Ka (12) Chicchan
Kablajuj (12) Kan

A single day may give you joy or disappoint, drive you mad or leave you feeling bored, but it's your overall lifespan that carries the frequencies of your soul's path, the currents of your sea. And so, as you contemplate the essence and progress of your life, the experiences you've had and the people you've met, ask Chicchan to lead you out of whatever confusion, clutter or cacophony may be present in your life right now, and use La Ka's powerful energies to redefine or redirect your horizon to the life you've always dreamed of but never thought you could attain. Then tune all of your mental, emotional and physical faculties to sail full speed toward it!

Oxlahun (13) Cimi
Oxlajuj (13) Kame

Close your journey through the Jaguar trecena with respect for and acceptance of yourself, your well-being and your potential. Embodying completion and the sacred *koyopa* essence of life, Oxlahun enriches the deep transformative powers of Cimi. Like a sacred waterfall of spirit, let these ancient energies bathe you with their blessing and soak all the way through to the marrow of your soul. The transition you seek is not a temporary state, but rather the next era in your personal evolution.

Manik' / Kej
Ruler of the Trecena
of Power and Respect

original artwork, printed here in black & white,
courtesy of Maree Gifkins

MANIK' / KEJ
The Trecena of Power and Respect

Manik', or Kej in K'iche' Maya, represents power, authority, respect, force, and hierarchy. This is the day of the *ajq'ijab'*—the Mayan priests—and represents the power inherent in religion. In fact, it's the nagual of the Mayan religion, as well as the rainforest, cacao beans, and all four-footed animals. Embodying stability and balance, Manik' is the nagual of the four cardinal points of the Earth and represents the four primary elements of earth, water, fire, and air. It also carries the four states of the human experience and the four colors of humanity: physical, emotional, mental, and spiritual, and the colors of yellow, white, red, and black. Manik's animal totem is the deer. In the Classical Maya tradition, it is associated with the cardinal direction West and the color black. In the tradition of modern-day K'iche' Maya, it is East and the color red. Manik' is also the most important of the four Year Bearers, which shape the nature and character of the solar years they are associated with.

On Manik' days, the Maya pray for harmony throughout the natural world and among all human beings—these are propitious days to ask for the strength to avoid betrayal and handle the difficulties in our lives. This is also an optimal time to find balance with the elements and to express gratitude for life. If you are able to spend Manik' days in nature, you can gain great power and energy.

Dignity, strength, humility and power. Respect, honor and integrity. These are the values Manik', the Deer, embodies. Free of the toxic effects of ego, Manik' stands head and shoulders above the skirmishes of mankind, the epitome of grace in the face of danger and uncertainty that's all around him. Profoundly spiritual and peaceful, Manik' seeks to impart no violence or harm to others, but does have the raw power to defend himself and others when the need arises. He is no gentle or weak spirit—he crushes the stereotype that spiritual beings are soft and passive. Indeed, the deepest spiritual thinkers and most balanced, confident individuals carry the greatest personal strength. And what is strength but the direct result of ultimate self-respect?

Real power comes from true respect. Not fear, not admiration or worship, not envy or insecurity. In modern society, many public and private figures carry an aura of apparent respect that in fact stands on a weak foundation: just think how easily a politician falls when it's discovered he's had an affair or has misappropriated public funds, how quickly a media celebrity goes out of favor once their sales start to sag. We are learning not to respect, but to want—we are taught to desire fame, money, status, influence, power—and eternal youth. These are the values celebrated by our media and our leaders. Respect for ourselves, for one another and our planet doesn't seem to have a seat at the table. This needs to change if we are going to live in a stable, sustainable and equitable world.

This trecena, your challenge is to find your strength. This doesn't mean ramping up your time at the gym or signing up for aikido. It means developing a stable, objective sense of self-respect, without the arrogance, judgment, and ego that often hang on to our psyches, latching on like psychic parasites. It means basing your sense of self and identity on your own thoughts and observations, not those of others. This applies to both negative and positive input—whether someone critizes or insults you, or praises or supports you. Your self-respect needs to be independent and free of external influence, for only then can you begin to extend true respect to others. And that's where real power is born. It's quiet and understated, but will last you a lifetime.

Respect who you are and what you do. Respect your talents and skills, respect the role you play in your family and society, and the legacy you will leave to future generations. Respect yourself, and live that respect through every pore of your being.

You will find that true respect, for yourself and others, does indeed build strength and power—the kind that will carry you through storm and upheaval, and enable you to stand on your own feet in the face of any challenge.

Hun (1) Manik'
Jun (1) Kej

Manik' holds profound respect for the spirituality present in all living things, but has no trouble expressing its raw, direct power. But with great power comes great responsibility, and to bear it well and with grace, you need a strong and stable foundation. Without it, your power will eventually drain and your responsibilities will overwhelm you.

Therein lies Manik's challenge for you today: to balance your power and confidence in yourself with humility, flexibility and understanding toward others.

Ka (2) Lamat
Kieb (2) Q'anil

Ka (Two) doubles the abundance and positive growth that Lamat brings in today. This gives you a powerful boost in whatever you aim to do—be it as simple as getting your grocery shopping or errands done quickly and effectively, or as demanding as figuring out the best configuration in your investment portfolio. But don't overreach or become overly ambitious—keep in mind that just as easily as you can duplicate today's energy, there is the equal possibility that you may fall into indecision if you take on too many goals or responsibilities.

Ox (3) Muluc
Oxib' (3) Toj

When a day sign or number carries difficult energies, we can generally rely on the other symbol's essence to balance or neutralize them. In the case of Ox Muluc, however, it's a bit more challenging, as both number and day sign are laden with some heavy energies. So if you do experience the impact of this pairing in a negative or unpleasant manner today, whether in the form of anxiety, fear, abuse, or, heaven forbid, anything worse, turn Ox's own energies to your favor by taking refuge in the three hearth stones Ox also represents—in other words, your home. This can be your physical home, or if that's not an option, your inner spiritual or emotional home. No matter how hard the energies assail you today, your inner home is impenetrable.

Kan (4) Oc
Kahib' (4) Tz'i

The power of authority of Oc buoyed by the power and authority of Manik' yields a blockbuster energy that commands ultimate respect. But rather than expend great effort to move mountains, you might instead reflect upon and recognize this power within you as it exists in its pure state. Commune with it in silence and tranquility, in meditation. This isn't control through fear, or enlightenment through ego. This is real power—power that empowers, authority that needs no police force.

Ho (5) Chuen
Job' (5) B'atz'

As the weaver's hand moves deftly across the loom, creating an intricate tapestry thread by thread, line by line, so Chuen weaves into the fabric of time the five stages of life that Ho symbolizes—childhood, youth, adulthood, mature adulthood, and elder. Whatever stage of life you are in, embrace, enjoy and honor the experience to its fullest, for it shall not come to pass again in this lifetime. Don't rush to grow out of one life era into the other, for you may regret not taking the time to enjoy and explore all that each one has to offer. Live life the way fruit ripens on trees: vibrant, alive and full of juice!

Uac (6) Eb
Wakib' (6) E'

Having a path to follow in life doesn't mean you can sit back and watch life happen. You cannot claim "destiny" or any sort of pre-ordained or divinely inspired order of events. Not only are you responsible for your actions and decisions, you bear a still greater responsibility: to choose the path you travel well. Today, seek the guidance of Uac and Manik' on your personal *saq b'e*, your life's journey: be strong, dignified and respect yourself. Seek practical, realistic solutions and approaches rather than denial, unrealistic expectations or escapist tendencies.

Uuc (7) Ben
Wukub' (7) Aj

It is at home, with our families, that the greatest discord often happens, as the usual veils of courtesy and diplomacy that shade us from each other's raw truth in public are left at the door. But it is also here, at home, that the deepest love, dignity and respect grow and take root. Uuc helps us see the varied and multitudinous facets of our innermost private lives, Ben guides and protects us, and the underlying current of Manik' grounds us, counteracting the potentially destabilizing force of Uuc. It is then up to each one of us to honor the power of these energies and apply them in good faith to our individual circumstances.

Uaxac (8) Ix
Wajxaqib' (8) I'x

Today, Ix the Jaguar walks the path of the mighty Stag. Charged with the raw power of Nature that he embodies, made all that more powerful by Manik's trecena, Ix weaves his way through the thick underbrush of life's jungles as Uaxac twists the sacred cord of time around his being. Track his knowing footsteps, follow his unique scent, spend time with him today, and you'll encounter the face of your own soul.

Connect with your source today, and every day—not just on Jaguar days.

Bolon (9) Men
B'elejeb' (9) Tz'ikin

Deep at the soul level, we all instinctively search for respect, dignity and inner peace. The things that fog our vision and shackle our wings are too many and too varied to list; but they are all of our own making. So today, soar high, high with Men, born on the ecstatic, exhilarating energy of Bolon, and release all of the weight you have been carrying; keep nothing with you as you rise. The higher you fly, the freer your mind and lighter your spirit. It is only in these divine heights that you can finally see the full essence and meaning of your life's journey.

Lahun (10) Cib
Lajuj (10) Ajmaq

If you, or some aspect of your life, is affected by your family's karmic past, your ancestral line, or the energies accumulated over many lifetimes in your family history, today is a great day to dissolve and dispel much of these issues. Cib opens the door to your family and ancestors, and Lahun strengthens bonds and relationships between people, making it easier for you to reach out to members of your family and heal long-standing emotional and psychic wounds, resolve issues, release resentments and forgive transgressions and misunderstandings.

Buluk (11) Caban
Junlajuj (11) No'j

Today, think for yourself. Let no one colonize your mind; no advertiser, no expert, no authority. In turn, do not attempt to influence others in the same way, regardless of how right you feel you are. Maintain a steady keel as you navigate the currents of today's waters. If you can remain neutral and free of judgment in your thoughts, the clarity of your perception and the depth of your understanding will intensify tenfold.

La Ka (12) Etznab
Kablajuj (12) Tijax

For the Maya, respect is one of the most important values in life. From respect stem all other positive, empowering forces: love, trust, self-esteem and confidence, to name a few. But for respect to thrive, truth must reign. So be honest with yourself. Call it like it is. Only when you accept full responsibility for your actions and decisions, past, present and future, can you embody the kind of rock-solid respect that your soul fully deserves—and in turn command it in all that you do in your life.

Oxlahun (13) Cauac
Oxlajuj (13) Kawoq

Like Bolon (9) Cauac, today is another example of the perfect fusion of Tzolk'in energies: the mystical Oxlahun, with its powerful connection to spiritual and psychic abilities, and the mysterious Cauac, with its profound connection to the Divine Feminine, merge into an energy cell several orders of magnitude more potent than either alone. If there were ever the chance to step into the eye of the hurricane and come out a more enlightened human being, this is it. Harness Cauac's and Oxlahun's all-seeing energies to peer deep into the underlying currents of your life and emerge with a wealth of life-changing awareness.

Ahau / Ajpu
Ruler of the Trecena of Illumination

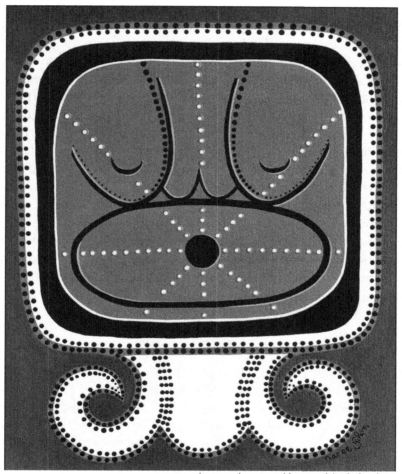

*original artwork, printed here in black & white,
courtesy of Maree Gifkins*

AHAU / AJPU
The Trecena of Illumination

Nagual of the sun, Ahau, or Ajpu in K'iche' Maya, epitomizes heroism in all of its forms—whether it's the legendary Hero Twins of the Mayan creation myths, physical victory in a battle or athletics competition, triumph over a mental or psychological challenge or issue, or conquering emotional struggle or pain. In line with these concepts, Ahau represents the blowgun hunter, the activity of hunting, death, and struggle; in fact, the glyph itself displays the face of the hunter with his lips pursed, ready to use the blowgun. This powerful day sign also symbolizes leadership and intuitive power, in their many forms: a chief or leader, a president, a CEO, a prophet, a spiritual warrior, psychic or diviner. On the negative side of heroism, Ahau represents hate, enmity, rage, and vengefulness. It is also the nagual and patron guardian of flowers, and governs solar and lunar eclipses. Ahau's animal totems are the eagle and the human being. In the Classical Maya tradition, it is associated with the cardinal direction South and the color yellow. In the tradition of modern-day K'iche' Maya, it is West and the color black.

On Ahau days, the Maya ask for wisdom, talent and physical strength and fortitude. Ahau helps us attain security and certainty, and to plan and achieve our goals and aspirations. This is the day of mental and psychological tests and challenges, and the day for Mayan ceremonies conducted to protect against *Wuqu' Qak'ix*, the seven sins of pride, ambition, envy, lies, crime, ingratitude, and ignorance through laziness. We should also honor departed grandparents and other ancestors.

Light is the ultimate source of all life. Born of the sun and the stars, Light cannot be seen yet illuminates all else. It exists both as waves and as particles, and is the fastest elemental force in the universe. It sets the standard and the benchmark for physical laws and for technologies that rely on speed. Light gives all of itself and asks nothing in return, an ever-flowing source of inspiration and insight, truth and clarity, art and creativity. It guides our spirit, infuses us with joy, and challenges us to take the highest path. Like the values and truths it embodies, Light allows for no excuses, no weakness, no failures of character or ability. While clouds on Earth and in our soul may dampen the strength, brilliance, and color of the light we see or feel, Light remains, always, the purest expression of itself and all that it illuminates.

In the Tzolk'in, Ahau is the Lord of Light, embodying the highest potential of all life and illuminating the sacred journeys of evolution of all living things. Your challenge in the trecena of Ahau is to purify your own inner light so that the path you travel may be clear and apparent. You may burn away the fog of uncertainty, fear, doubt, and superstition, but the real test comes in not allowing them to return. Ask Ahau to guide you through your hardest times, your toughest challenges. Rather than allowing ego, fear, insecurity or other toxic or deceptive emotions or traits steer you down the wrong path, seek the higher road, let the light of your soul illuminate the specific situation you face—and have the courage to stand up to it, resolve it, conquer whatever fears, anxieties or harm it is causing you. Don't darken your spirit with weakness, laziness, or evasion, and do not allow others to sway you off course, for no matter how right they may appear to be, no matter how vehemently they may argue, the choice and the struggle are yours and yours alone.

The toughest battles are those fought solo, in the deep interiors of the soul, not on the battlefield. The more open you are to your own inner light, the more you trust the blinding power of this inexorable natural force, the sooner you will attain the truths you seek. Remember that darkness is the absence of light, light is not the absence of darkness.

All of the Earth's peoples, cultures, and races have turned their faces to the sun since the beginning of time; in fact, so have all living things. Deep within all that lives, lies an innate biological and spiritual instinct to touch the Sun. There is perhaps nothing more natural than for Life to align with Light in a sacred dance of co-existence and co-creation.

Follow the path of Ahau, and sail your ship into the sunlit horizon of your soul.

Hun (1) Ahau
Jun (1) Ajpu

This is a time of bold, visionary thinking, resolve and willpower, and firm courage in the face of difficulty. Each day of this trecena can shed light on something of importance to you, something you're dealing with or need to address; use the illuminating essence of Ahau and the spark-plug firepower of Hun to ignite a trecena-long journey of triumphs over all that restricts and binds you, all that ails, threatens or harms you, all that holds you back from your full potential.

Ka (2) Imix
Kieb (2) Imox

There is an eternal dichotomy in our world that permeates all aspects of life and consciousness: day/night, light/dark, male/female, yin/yang, hot/cold, life/death, good/bad, right/wrong, left/right, and so on. When you look a little beyond the surface of things, as Imix does, you'll see hints of this polarity everywhere, in countless forms and iterations. This can be either reassuring or unnerving, depending on your state of mind, what you're looking at or listening to, and many other factors. That's the challenge of Imix and Ka. But remember the final choice is always yours: you determine how to navigate your own reality.

Ox (3) Ik'
Oxib' (3) Iq'

Uncertainty and indecisiveness in the face of an already fickle current of energies can easily result in very misguided actions. So be mindful throughout the day about where Ox and Ik' seem to be taking you: don't place great stock in feelings of uncertainty, doubt or fear, or unusually intense sensations of ambition, importance or popularity—and certainly do not act on them. Rather, wait till the next day to think more clearly, practically and positively.

Kan (4) Akb'al
Kahib' (4) Aq'ab'al

If you have been feeling incomplete and unrealized, know you are already whole and complete, for at the soul level time is irrelevant—and time is the one reality of the human experience that causes so much frustration. Those aspects of your life's journey that have not yet materialized, are already there, but still in their potential form. Continue on your path, aware and awake, and the seeds of your future will germinate.

Ho (5) Kan
Job' (5) K'at

Modern society has embedded in us this inexplicable drive of "getting there first." And so we all dutifully apply ourselves in life and work, trying to be the first to have achieved "something," whatever it may be. Ho can certainly help get you there "first" or to be "ahead of your time," but do take the time to plan and think through your intended path—especially on a day like today. A Kan day isn't quite so straightforward; it requires a deeper understanding of its complex energies to harness its true power. Sit with Kan for a bit today, and then open the floodgates for Ho.

Uac (6) Chicchan
Wakib' (6) Kan

There are certain core realities that impact the well-being of any family, regardless of culture, religion, ethnicity or political system. These realities include physical and mental health, dignified employment, access to resources, property and strong, stable interpersonal relations. The problem of course is that in today's world, few can escape the constant onslaught of issues and challenges that make achieving true well-being for ourselves and our families tough. All Uac (6) days will support your efforts to stabilize your personal or family environment, but with Chicchan on board, today is particularly powerful to ask for vitality, clarity, and understanding in your life, and to neutralize fear and anxiety that may be holding you or your family back.

Uuc (7) Cimi
Wukub' (7) Kame

Remember that for something new to thrive, the old must die: thought patterns, emotional reactions, perceptions of reality. Let go of your old, stagnant or unhealthy habits so that you can embrace more enlightened, empowered ways of living and thinking. Easier said than done... old habits have this way of anchoring roots deep in your psyche, so you've got work to do!

This is the challenge that Cimi and Uuc present to you today. Will you take them up on it?

Uaxac (8) Manik'
Wajxaqib' (8) Kej

To handle the difficulties and challenges in your life, ask for strength and stability. You cannot resolve anything if you're unbalanced, weak, insecure or out of sync with your soul. So let Uaxac, the cord of time, weave a double-sided canvas to support and empower you, and Manik' uphold the pillars of your universe with harmony, stability and power. Stand tall and powerful in the face of all your adversaries, be they internal or external; familiar or foreign; mental, emotional or physical.

Bolon (9) Lamat
B'elejeb' (9) Q'anil

Today brings in a wonderfully joyous, celebratory energy that is just perfect for birthdays and birth announcements, weddings and engagement parties, anniversaries, graduations and other significant life events. If you celebrate your event today, not only does it have a high chance of going extremely well; it is also likely to produce a lasting swell of abundance, prosperity and fruitfulness.

Lahun (10) Muluc
Lajuj (10) Toj

By natural law, life is full of highs and lows, which we have to learn to navigate in order to achieve the balance and harmony we all instinctively seek. Today, Lahun accentuates the trials and tests that Ahau's trecena throws down on the table, but also joins forces with Muluc to show you the golden middle path toward resolution and advancement. So whatever challenge or apparent obstacle you are facing right now, trust in Lahun and Muluc to help you see through the noise and distraction of the immediate difficulty, and focus on the long-term horizon. Remember the best way out of any tough spot is not around but through.

Buluk (11) Oc
Junlajuj (11) Tz'i

In this trecena, Ahau tests your mental, psychological and physical fortitude—and therein lies the core of your personal authority. Use the energies of Oc to embrace the tests and challenges you face today with an even keel, a cool head, a firm resolve, knowing that all this represents the totality of your past, present and future. All that you learn, all that you are forced to deal with, all that challenges your status quo and your comfort level, these are the things that are your greatest teachers and your truest allies.

La Ka (12) Chuen
Kablajuj (12) B'atz'

The colorful thread that weaves individual life experiences into one great tapestry of human evolution is made of the brilliant light of consciousness. And it's Chuen who spins this thread for each one of us. So as we reflect upon our lives today, as we should every La Ka day, let us recognize the profound interconnectedness of the people, events, and situations that shape our experience of life on this planet. The more we treat each person, event, and situation with honor and respect, and the less we expect in return, the more enlightened and evolved we become.

Choose your threads wisely when you weave the tapestry of your life.

Oxlahun (13) Eb
Oxlajuj (13) E'

Physicists now believe the future may influence the present... and that means your destiny, which remains your choice and your will, can indeed impact your present life. If you accept this strange premise, you can pull your destiny closer to you, right now, perhaps by bending the path of your soul's journey out of linear time, as if twisting it into a spiritual Moebius strip.

That is the challenge for today!

Ben / Aj
Ruler of the Trecena of Guidance

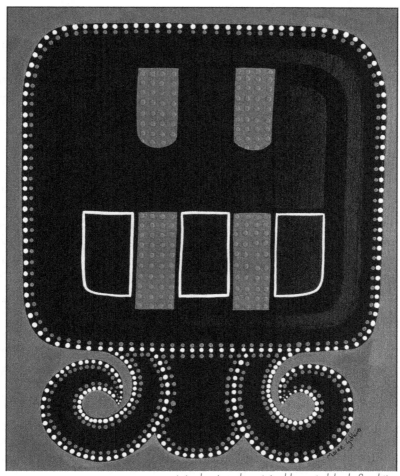

original artwork, printed here in black & white,
courtesy of Maree Gifkins

BEN / AJ
The Trecena of Guidance

Ben, or Aj in K'iche' Maya, symbolizes the guiding light of family and home, and the tenderness and innocence of small children. It represents sugar cane, corn and the growth, health and abundance of offspring, seeds and crops in general; renewal and restoration; stability, strength and solidity; and resoluteness of character. It watches over professions, vocations and trades, and symbolizes the staff of authority and power. It symbolizes clairvoyance and telepathy, sacred speech and dreams, and connects cosmic and telluric energies. As the nagual of the home and children, Ben has a strong connection with the nourishment, renewal, and flourishing of all things related to home and household—be it human, plant or animal. In short, Ben embodies the energy and vitality of life itself. Ben's animal totems are the armadillo and the bee. In the Classical Maya tradition, it is associated with the cardinal direction East and the color red. In the tradition of modern-day K'iche' Maya, it is North and the color white.

On Ben days, the Maya give thanks for their children, their lives and their homes. They ask for good food and the protection of their homes, crops, gardens, and animals, as well as their physical, mental, and professional wellbeing. Ben days bring good weather and good harvests, and facilitate the return home.

The discovery of the Americas in the 15th century, the Industrial Revolution in the 18th and 19th centuries, and globalization in our current lifetime, have all driven the expansion of minds and markets. We can live, work, and travel virtually anywhere we like. We can enjoy food from all over the world in our own homes or down the street, listen to music of any genre or culture delivered instantly to our desktop for mere pennies, talk to friends and relatives no matter where they are in the world, and hold virtual meetings in multiple time zones simultaneously. We call ourselves "global citizens" and think nothing of moving every few years to other cities, states or even other countries. It's all part of modern living.

So where is home? Is it where we live physically now, or is it where we grew up or where we end up retiring? Perhaps a more appropriate question is, *what* is home? The specific definition of "home" depends on the culture and/or faith you've grown up with, but in its full essence and meaning, home is your onion. At its core, it's that place deep inside your soul that's the source of your inner happiness and stability, the little fire that gives you direction in life. Once you've got it, no one can take it away from you. Your house can burn down, your city can be destroyed in an earthquake, everything can be taken away from you, but your inner home is unassailable.

It is imperative to your inner peace and stability that you strengthen and fireproof this core. Do not allow events, situations, news reports, or the toxic emotions of others to seep into your core and poison your mind and soul. It may seem a little selfish, a little callous at first, but if you really wish to help others, your spiritual and psychological base needs to be strong and unbiased. It's tough love for the soul!

Working outwards from the onion's core, are all of your other homes. Your emotional or sentimental home, the family or personal environment in which you live, the physical structure that houses you and your belongings, the community you are a part of, your faith or religion, your culture, your country, your planet. You may have few or many of these secondary or external homes, but we each have an inner core that we need to keep healthy, happy, and strong—for otherwise, all of our other homes will wither and dim.

It is equally important to recognize cracks in the various layers of the onion. If your home and/or your family suffocates you, puts you down, doesn't let you breathe free or tries to influence or control you, you need to claim your psychic and emotional space. The closer the issue in question lies to the core of your onion, the more challenging it is to resolve, yet the more significant—and often urgent.

This trecena, stay home with Ben. Enjoy the company of your loved ones, give thanks for their presence in your life and the blessings they bring. If it's just you, rejoice in the wonderful richness your mind, body, and soul have to offer you. Above all, enjoy your onion.

Hun (1) Ben
Jun (1) Aj

Start Ben's trecena with a small personal ceremony or morning meditation to offer your thanks and gratitude for your home, your family, and especially your children if you're a parent. Nurture an atmosphere of tranquility, contentment and joy in your home, so that you and your family may have a sacred sanctuary to protect you from the stresses of the external world. At the core of your home is your own internal inner peace. Honor that inner home, that part of your soul that powers your waking consciousness and all other aspects of your life.

Ka (2) Ix
Kieb (2) I'x

Honor the many colors and aspects of your life today: your life at home, your life at work, your life at school, your life in public or in the community... all the places and all the circles you inhabit and influence. But no matter how far you travel or how long you're away, remember your inner home is always where the soul is. Nurture that inner peace and vitality that will, in turn, harmonize all of your external worlds. If you can embrace this duality of awarenesss and experience, your life will be made whole.

Ox (3) Men
Oxib' (3) Tz'ikin

Let the Eagle lift you up from any doubts or fears you may be feeling about your life, and fly straight into the face of your personal challenges. 'Tis a heady flight, fraught with gusting tempers, ego extremes and malfunctioning arguments. But take heart! As the ruling day sign of this trecena, Ben sends a homing beacon through the fog of uncertainty that Ox creates, guiding Men to fly home as if by a powerful inner navigation. Indeed, sooner or later even the mightiest of eagles must come home to their nests and recoup their energy and stamina.

Kan (4) Cib
Kahib' (4) Ajmaq

The souls of our ancestors and those of our future children live in the same place: the deep dark blue night of potential past and future. Yet they both have a profound influence over our lives—one calling in from the past to share wisdom and advice we can apply in our present lifetime, the other radiating upon us from the future, admonishing us to make the right choices and do the right thing in the present.

Honor your ancestors and your children.

Ho (5) Caban
Job' (5) No'j

Dedicate your mental faculties to your home today—your interior design skills, your sense of style, your organizational ability. Clear away clutter, put the dishes away, tidy up, rearrange furniture, organize items in closets and drawers. Think about the way you run the household and see if there is any room for improvement or to become more efficient and effective so you have more personal time. But be sure to do all this for you and your family, not simply to be clean and organized. Your home should feel and look like not just a home, but *your* home.

Uac (6) Etznab
Wakib' (6) Tijax

Whatever ails you or your loved ones, whether physically, emotionally or psychically, today's energies give you a rock-solid foundation to stand on and ensure a safe, nurturing environment for healing. Yet this doesn't mean we should pamper or pity those who need our help, as Etznab teaches us—sometimes, as the saying goes, *truth hurts*. Ultimately however, that's the only thing that can ever truly resolve an issue or ailment: raw, naked reality. As long as you have the security of your own stable inner core, you'll be able to *handle the truth*.

Be the beacon of stability for you and your family.

Uuc (7) Cauac
Wukub' (7) Kawoq

It's often in the midst of a rainstorm that you find the greatest inner peace, or that insight or inspiration you were looking for... for rainstorms wash away everything but the source. With Uuc's ability to see things from all angles and Cauac's sweeping, massive force, your soul gets a power-wash today. Everything that has ever held you back is blasted away: all the layers of self-deception, insecurity, weakness, and fear, all the dirt and grime of guilt and shame, all the toxins of others' poisons. The onslaught isn't easy to take, especially if you've got a lot of layers built up—and it may take a few rounds of the Tzolk'in; but trust the energies to do their job and you'll come out squeaky clean.

Uaxac (8) Ahau
Wajxaqib' (8) Ajpu

An especially critical day for completion, resolution and closing. Don't walk away from something you've started or someone you've committed to, just because things are tougher. That's when you learn what you're made of. So strengthen your resolve, draw on your roots of home and family that Ben's trecena empowers now, and harness the highly charged solar energy of Ahau to push forward and pull through whatever difficulties you're dealing with in your life.

Bolon (9) Imix
B'elejeb' (9) Imox

When storms rage outside, there is no better place than home, warmed by the fire and our mother's reassuring embrace. So too we seek refuge in the comfort of our familiar thought patterns and reactions when people, life events or situations attack our sense of reality. But just as all babies must one day leave the secure warmth of their mother's womb, so too must we all face our toughest challenges in order to evolve and advance on our soul journey. Today is a great day to be psychically reborn: Bolon's strong, positive energy softens Imix's impact and guides you toward your life's purpose.

Lahun (10) Ik'
Lajuj (10) Iq'

Time to take care of the home front today—literally and figuratively. Lahun helps you nurture the bonds and relationships among your family members, providing stability and cooperation, while Ik' enables you to cleanse and purify any misunderstandings, resentments, or recent quarrels, refreshing our relations with new perspectives. Our time on this planet is short, and Lahun days remind us to enjoy the time we do have with those we love, for that is the most treasured of all.

Buluk (11) Akb'al
Junlajuj (11) Aq'ab'al

Nurture your inner home, the hearth of your soul. This is where the source of your power lies, the core of your life's purpose. Honor and respect it, for it is truly sacred. You are the only one who can guard the integrity of your soul.

Today is also a good day to ground yourself, to take care of house, home, and family. If you have children, take a little time to talk to them about the sacred seeds of potential they hold within them. Tell them how important it is to love and never to give up on their own promise. A child is like the bud of an infinitely blooming flower, season after season, layer upon layer, the seeds blossom and bear fruit; but to do so, the flower needs the sun and water of self-love and self-respect.

La Ka (12) Kan
Kablajuj (12) K'at

Today, express gratitude for those aspects and elements of your life you have been able to enrich, evolve or enlighten during this trecena, the oppressive patterns of the past you have been able to break, and new seeds you have been able to plant. Wherever you may be in your lifetime, draw on your life experience, the momentum of your karma, and your insight into the soul of things to drive the positive change you want to see in your life, your family, and relationships, your country, community, or the world in general.

Oxlahun (13) Chicchan
Oxlajuj (13) Kan

Today is one of the most powerful days in the Tzolk'in. Oxlahun, the most profound and mystical number of the calendar, intertwines its intense psychic energies with the resplendent inner fire of Chicchan, one of the most profound and mystical day signs of the calendar. This is the day to nourish your *koyopa*, your kundalini, the vital energy coursing through your mind, body and soul. Let nothing divert you from this sacred communion: retain your humility, grace and integrity, and maintain purity of intention as you express the power of this great ancient energy in your life and the lives of those around you.

CIMI / KAME
RULER OF THE TRECENA OF TRANSFORMATION

original artwork, printed here in black & white,
courtesy of Maree Gifkins

CIMI / KAME
The Trecena of Transformation

Cimi, or Kame in K'iche' Maya, means "death" and "rebirth"; grammatically, *kame* is the present tense of "the eternal Now." Cimi represents Xib'alb'a, the Underworld of Mayan mythology, and embodies the eternal flow and cycle of death, rebirth and transformation. The Maya did, and still do believe in reincarnation; Cimi is the day sign that embodies this transcendental spiritual state. It carries a special connection to the world of the ancestors, and is embued with plentiful feminine energy, which render Cimi days excellent for resolving marital conflict. Cimi also signifies fortitude; humility and obedience; scorn, contempt, and clumsiness. Cimi's animal totem is the owl. In the Classical Maya tradition, it is associated with the cardinal direction North and the color white. In the tradition of modern-day K'iche' Maya, it is South and the color yellow.

On Cimi days, the Maya pray for long life, for the delay or removal of death, and for rest and peace for those departing this world. It is a special day to contact our ancestors, communicate with higher beings or other dimensions, and access spiritual knowledge. Cimi is also a good day for healing, especially serious illnesses, protecting travelers, preventing accidents, and washing away negative energies.

In the Western/Northern mind, death is typically associated with the tragic end of a life, something most of us generally fear; it has therefore become a profoundly frightening concept. This is one of the primary reasons we worship youth and neglect our elders; our focus is on the fruit-producing flowers of our society. For the Maya however, death is a part of and complements life. It carries positive, beneficent energy that brings us peace and harmony, and allows the spirit to regenerate and return again to life. It is, in a word, transformational. Death transcends Life so that Life may transcend Death. This is the perpetual dance of intertwined duality that mirrors the everpresent cyclical nature of all things. Virtually every aspect of existence has its yin and its yang: the one cannot be without the other.

In the Mayan worldview, the nature of Time is cyclical rather than linear, organic rather than structured, multidimensional rather than single-tracked. As scholar Martin Prechtel explains, the Present is the world center, the *axis mundi*. The Past, which embodies all that has been, and the Future, which embodies all that is yet to come, are anchored to the center tree of the Eternal Now. This is the reason why so many spiritual teachings focus on the "now" moment—the present already envelops the past and future.

All that we do in our lives, all of the thoughts we think, the emotions we feel, the words we speak, the actions we take, feed our future Past and generate the legacy we leave to our families, the rest of humanity and our civilization's history. This is why Cimi, and our resonance with its energy, is so critical to our individual and collective futures. We transform the energies of our ancestors and our parents into new actions and new experiences that become our lives and our memories, and our children in turn transform our energies into their own lives.

This trecena, open up to the possibility of change, of transformation. Release the asphyxiating chains of fear, anxiety, and uncertainty, and slip into the warm energetic pool of your soul's true promise and potential. Cimi is so potent that it can bring wildly different energies into people's lives on the same day; how it manifests, in what specific form or in what specific outcome, will depend on your individual path and mindset. This is true of all the day signs in the Tzolk'in, but particularly so with Cimi. This is why it is so important to stay open and free, and not to suffocate any aspect of your life with worries, fears, or any other toxic emotions or thoughts. Embrace, instead, the changes and transitions in your life, be they changes in lifestyle, work, relationships, moving to a new place, or simply entering a new decade. Kiss the past with a goodbye of gratitude and embrace the future with the excitement of a child.

Indeed... as the Maya might say if they spoke Latin: *carpe diem! Seize the day (sign)!*

Hun (1) Cimi
Jun (1) Kame

Celebrate the cycles of life, death, and rebirth; of beginnings, closings and re-openings; of the new, the old and the remade; of the past, present and future. What is dying, shall be reborn. What is toxic, shall be purified. What causes pain, shall be resolved. What is imprisoned, shall be set free.

These are the eternal cycles of all that is, above and below, within and without, from the impossibly vast universe to the quantum particles that may or may not be whispering in your ear at this very moment...

Ka (2) Manik'
Kieb (2) Kej

Today, Ka presents you with two options, two choices, two paths that diverge. Before you make your decision, remember that one choice does not have to exclude or oppose the other; it may instead complement and fufill. The final outcome depends on your will and intention. The mighty Manik' will carry your decision through with force and authority, so weigh your options with great care today, and make the right decision for the right reasons.

Ox (3) Lamat
Oxib' (3) Q'anil

Although Lamat days are typically auspicious for planting new seeds, the incongruous energy of Ox (Three) throws a stone into the crystalline pool of abundance and growth. This means you need to choose the seeds that you plant today, carefully. You still have a powerful, positive energy on your side, but there is no telling how the day will turn out—you may experience doubt, uncertainty, or insecurity about some aspect of your actions or thoughts, or run a certain degree of risk. The key is to remain strong and confident, and steer Lamat clear of Ox's wavering path.

Kan (4) Muluc
Kahib' (4) Toj

Today, Muluc, the nagual of Water and Fire, melts together with Kan, the number that represents all four elements. This generates double Water energy and double Fire energy. Rather than pulling out your survival kit and running for the hills, however, take some time today to honor and give thanks for the two archetypal embodiments of water and fire: first in their form as sacred elements in rituals and ceremonies, and second as essential resources for life—whether as clean drinking water or rain for your garden; and as heat for cooking or energy for so many of our modern conveniences.

Ho (5) Oc
Job' (5) Tz'i

You are part of a greater, deeper, more ancient whole. This is why no one can take your own dignity away. No one can commandeer your thoughts, no one can own your heart, no one can impose false laws onto your soul. If so many of us are disconnected from each other, it's only because we have forgotten how to sing to one another, how to listen, how to talk, without judgment, comparison, false intentions or fear. Let these dry old shells that we wear die and our joyous, youthful souls spring back to vibrant life!

Uac (6) Chuen
Wakib' (6) B'atz'

For many of us, life is a complex web of unending tasks and responsibilities, dreams and wishes, goals and ambitions. Yet the more technology, tools, and resources we have, the more complicated our lives seem to become. Chuen is the weaver of time and the multitasker of the Tzolk'in—let him help you handle the multitudinous menu of your daily life, but skip the short attention span he tends to have! He may manipulate a great diversity of threads in his tapestry, but it is only with focus and discipline that those threads materialize into solid reality—and that's where practically minded Uac comes in. Ground Chuen's chaos, and you've got gold.

Uuc (7) Eb
Wukub' (7) E'

Just as the path you travel in life is not one but many, so there is not one but many endings, and therefore many new beginnings as well. Indeed, there are pathways within pathways, beginnings within beginnings, endings within endings... and so on and on in a breathtaking orchestra of living experience. Enjoy and learn from each journey you make, to the very fullest—from the momentous transatlantic voyages to the impromptu daytrips, from sweeping life changes to the little illuminations as you sit at a traffic light.

Uaxac (8) Ben
Wajxaqib' (8) Aj

Respect and Gratitude never go out of style. For the Maya, these are cornerstone values that form the basis of healthy, lasting human relationships and communities. Sadly, over the course of the past several decades they have been bled out of our busy "modern society" life through a long-standing, insistent, incessant focus on consumption, instant gratification, and financial success. But that can be changed—starting with each one of us. Be grateful for the lives and fortunes of your loved ones, respect your children as much as your elders, and maintain your personal inner peace.

Bolon (9) Ix
B'elejeb' (9) I'x

If you are pregnant or desire to become pregnant, devote time today to sacred meditation for your unborn child. If you already have children, honor their innocence and purity; treat them with respect, fairness and dignity, for they embody your own essence. Ix embodies the vital spirit of all life, and Bolon is associated with pregnancy and the process of human gestation and development—their energies intertwined, they present to you a powerful and extremely propitious day to honor your children, born and unborn.

Lahun (10) Men
Lajuj (10) Tz'ikin

Like many other singularly powerful forces of nature, Men, the Eagle, flies alone. But the Eagle, too, belongs to its own clan, its own kind. It is this belonging to a family, a community, a species, that inspires, that makes us soar and strive for greater things—and leave an active legacy for our race and our planet. Let us all not only pursue our individual goals and dreams, but seek a higher, deeper, smarter collective evolution so that the human experience on this planet can truly mean something.

Let us all be an Eagle.

Buluk (11) Cib
Junlajuj (11) Ajmaq

Go deeper still with Cib and the great power of Buluk, dive far into the vast ocean depths of your family's past to understand the underlying currents and energies that influence your lifetime and life journey. If you can come to understand and accept the psychic legacy of your blood line, without judgment and without condemnation, you will cleanse your karma and clear your lifepath for your own evolution.

La Ka (12) Caban
Kablajuj (12) No'j

La Ka represents the totality of one's lifetime, the sum total of all actions and experiences. In the context of Cimi's connection to the ancestral line and Caban's deep introspection, this energy is massively amplified and needs to be honored today.

In order to understand the different parts and pieces of your life and your relationships, you need freedom and tranquility. You need your time alone. So take it, for yourself, guilt-free. Step off the treadmill of responsibility to others, and enjoy the inner space that is yours and yours alone... and always will be.

Oxlahun (13) Etznab
Oxlajuj (13) Tijax

Plug into the powerful energies of Oxlahun and its innate connection to the sacred *koyopa* soulfire, married today with Etznab's profound healing powers, to rebalance and purify your mind and body, on the elemental, psychic, and soul level, for that is where the ultimate core of all illness and suffering lies. Reach deep through whatever ails or hurts you, to the source of your illness or pain. But it is not enough to dispel—to complete your healing, commit to accepting direct and personal responsibility for your own well-being henceforth.

Cauac / Kawoq
Ruler of the Trecena of Rainstorms

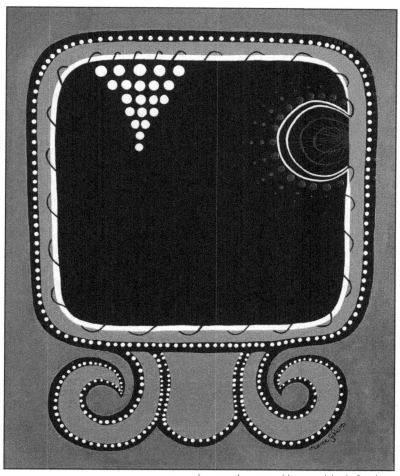

original artwork, printed here in black & white,
courtesy of Maree Gifkins

CAUAC / KAWOQ
The Trecena of Rainstorms

The Divine Feminine. That is the crowning energy that Cauac, or Kawoq in K'iche' Maya, carries. Given its special connection with women and feminine energy, Cauac represents women in all their roles and walks of life, especially as mothers, wives, sisters, midwives, and healers. This is a powerful sign that channels massive volumes of energy and force: it symbolizes spiritual connection, contact and communication; blood lightning signals and messages; difficulty, curses, and sacrifice; spiritual unrest and mental conflict and weakness. It is connected to the forces of nature, signifying thunder, lightning, and all manner of powerful rainstorms—typhoons, cyclones and hurricanes. It is also the archetype of community and communities, in all senses of the word, from family to neighborhood to city to nation to society and culture, and symbolizes our relationship with everyone and everything around us. Cauac is the nagual and patron of midwives, and is sometimes said to represent the celestial home of the gods. Curiously, it is also the nagual of all kinds of disputes. Cauac's animal totems are the turtle and the puma. In the Classical Maya tradition, it is associated with the cardinal direction West and the color black. In the tradition of modern-day K'iche' Maya, it is East and the color red.

On Cauac days, the *ajq'ijab'* (Mayan priests) and the *k'exelon* (midwives) burn copal to ask for the well-being of their communities, and the people pray for everpresent harmony in their home lives and among their friends. This is a highly auspicious day for all matters related to health, healing and well-being. It is also the day for quartz crystals and the sacred tz'ite seeds Maya Daykeepers use in their readings.

Rainstorms bring forth the blessings of life-giving waters, of warmth and comfort, abundant harvests and growth, but also the potential for torrential downpours, sweeping winds, and floods that can erode entire cities, relationships, or histories. Like the Sun, the Ocean, or the Wind, Cauac propels great amounts of energy and force—it is a vital source sign that will put you face to face with your own personal rainstorms.

This trecena, leave your umbrella at home. Step outside as you are and let Cauac's rain seep deep into the marrow of your soul. Let it dissolve your worries and anxieties, flush out your fears, wash away toxic emotions and thoughts. Let it comfort your heart, soothe your mind, clear the path you walk. Above all, accept Cauac with all of its power—the power to nourish exuberant, abundant life, and the power to flood, destroy, and overpower. Such is the everpresent duality in all aspects of existence; denying it only delays the fulfillment we seek. However strongly we may desire only the best experiences or participate in only certain tasks and responsibilities—usually that which is easier or more enjoyable—we need to recognize the natural harmony and balance between two of everything. Human society needs both women and men; day cannot exist without night; life without death would spiral into madness. There can be no endless growth, whether in nature or the economy. The cycles of sustainability, balance, and harmony are woven into the very fabric of reality—and no amount of marketing, money, or media noise can change that. The sooner we all accept and embrace the natural state of things, the more we respect our power as human beings and the power of nature, the sooner we shall find ourselves on the path we seek.

These are the vast and overwhelming forces of nature, whether human, animal, or planetary, at once simple and complex, violent and compassionate, that meander and swell, deplete and nurture. Respect their power and their fragility, their strength and their softness. They are a part of you as they are a part of all existence.

This is what creates, in the end, true community. We may all be individuals living independent lives, but we are part of various groups and communities, from our family and the place we live, to our country and global human society. Tying it all together is Cauac's distinctly feminine energy, for, as author Ken Johnson explains, "The sense of community and communion is founded in the feminine principle." So honor the women in your family and your community, honor that nurturing, bonding energy that keeps everyone and everything together in the face of the most violent storms.

The power of Cauac is unlike that of any other... so use it well. Respect and honor it, harness it with the purest of intentions. It will return the favor a thousandfold.

Hun (1) Cauac
Jun (1) Kawoq

Cauac's first soft, warm droplets fall onto your face, inspiring the first gush of intent, the first rivulet of determination, the first wave of action. Trust the impetus of Hun and the raw power of Cauac to deliver you to the place you need to be to realize the full extent of your dreams. But it is up to you to harness and shape their intertwined energies, and give meaning and substance to the rainstorm you generate. Will it be a soft spring rain to infuse life into your orchards, or will it be a hurricane of unstoppable force?

Ka (2) Ahau
Kieb (2) Ajpu

In every battle, there are at least two opponents. In every conflict, you need something or someone to resist or fight against, otherwise there simply is no conflict. It's the push-pull duality of heaven & earth, mind & body, freedom & constraint. As you navigate clashes between opposing sides, differing opinions, or conflicting situations, pull in Ahau's piercing intuition and Cauac's healing powers to calm Ka's polarizing energy. Listen without judgment or ego, and you will know how to strike the balance.

Ox (3) Imix
Oxib' (3) Imox

Ooh, better stay home today—in fact, lock the door! Ox mixes it up with Imix, an explosive combination that might just blow a few psychic fuses out there. When uncertainty, obstruction and risk enter the alternate streams of consciousness that Imix carries, there's no telling where you'll end up.

But that's if you're unprepared. For all of you rock-climbing, bungee-jumping Type A's, this is the perfect day to go brave the perfect psychic storm. The forecast is, after all, in your favor: it's Cauac's trecena. Just be sure to take your survival kit with you.

Kan (4) Ik'
Kahib' (4) Iq'

Today Ik' connects with the moon and the air, with a feminine energy that makes all things whole and complete. Whether you know it or not, deep within at the level of your soul, you too are complete. Draw on this well of power to pull your consciousness closer to your higher self, and to clear your soul and psyche of anger, resentment, envy, depression, and other stagnant or negative energies.

Ho (5) Akb'al
Job' (5) Aq'ab'al

Be the dreamer of the night who calls in the first rays of the morning light. Be the void that gives birth to promise and potential. Be the song that gives voice to the words inside your soul. This is the time for the birth of the ideas, thoughts and intentions that have been developing in the warm dark night of your subconcious, for preparing them for the metamorphosis into action and reality.

Uac (6) Kan
Wakib' (6) K'at

Release yourself from the prisons you've built around and for your mind, body and soul, untangle the heavy nets binding your ability to dream, and heal those deep wounds that still lie raw hidden beneath years of pain, fear and trauma. This, more than any wishful thinking, more than any coming "conscious enlightenment," more than any closing date in the Mayan Long Count calendar, will set you free.

Do you truly want to be free? Then *you* need to do the work, for you're the only one who can free you.

Uuc (7) Chicchan
Wukub' (7) Kan

YOU are responsible for your own destiny. You alone hold the reins to your life path. No matter what you've been through, or who's put you through it, ultimately it is you who hold the upper hand in every aspect of your life. You alone sit on top of your mountain, able to see the vast horizon of your soul at 360 degrees, able to feel the full range of human experience—and deciding what kind of life you really want. It's just a matter of shifting your perceptions, ways of thinking, reactions, habits, assumptions. Tough? Yes, very. But it's extraordinarily empowering.

Uaxac (8) Cimi
Wajxaqib' (8) Kame

The sacred, mystical cycle of life, death, and rebirth. Each night we sleep, we die; each day we wake, we are reborn. So does Uaxac's cord of time twist along the path of eternity that Cimi embodies; use it as a guide, a lifeline as you work through life transitions or transformations. Never forget that deep, strong connection with your bloodline, your family karma, your elders, who guide, support and protect you at every turn... they're there, always, no matter how alone you feel.

As the tides ebb and flow over sand, so the currents of our lives move with the rhythms of the vast ocean of collective consciousness.

Bolon (9) Manik'
B'elejeb' (9) Kej

What is life worth living if not to its fullest, deepest, most painfully beautiful? Through your soul courses the blood of a mighty stag. Let it run free.

Bolon rains a golden waterfall of pure power onto the great Manik'. Tilt your head back and let your soul flood with its fiercely positive energy! Today you are crowned guardian of the forest.

Lahun (10) Lamat
Lajuj (10) Q'anil

Feminine energy abounds today, generating vast volumes of fertility, abundance and prosperity. Nestled in the warm, nourishing bosom of Cauac, Lamat and Lahun relax and enrich the mind and body, recharge the spirit, and strengthen the bonds and relationships between people. Stop for a moment during your busy day, and take the time to soak in these powerful rejuvenating energies. They will heal, recharge and replenish your source essence—this is especially important if you are a parent, teacher, caregiver, or in the medical profession.

Buluk (11) Muluc
Junlajuj (11) Toj

Buluk is a force of nature. Incredibly powerful, headstrong, inimitable, it chooses no sides and can therefore cause great good or great harm. Muluc, too, is a vital force that gives back much more than it receives, and embodies both the highest grace and the lowest abuses human beings are capable of. Together, Buluk and Muluc whip up a powerstorm of energy and potential that requires tremendous strength of will and character to navigate and maneuver. In time, as this combination repeats each Tzolk'in round, you can learn how to harness these energies for a positive outcome—but it does take time.

La Ka (12) Oc
Kablajuj (12) Tz'i

True spiritual authority cannot be realized until you have accounted for and accepted as yours all of your actions and experiences, discovered and recognized your life's path and purpose, and attained harmony and equilibrium within your soul. The energy of La Ka (Twelve), which represents the totality of one's life, helps you in your quest. Today is only one day; your spiritual path lasts a lifetime, so use days like these for small quantum leaps forward. Remember there are no deadlines for your soul's journey.

Oxlahun (13) Chuen
Oxlajuj (13) B'atz'

Oxlahun and Chuen celebrate the extraordinary ability of the human being and the human body to express emotion and thought through movement, creativity, and intention, and to develop powerful spiritual and psychic abilities. This is a time to play, explore, dance, and celebrate simply being alive. It's in pure egoless innocent joy that evolution accelerates. But to do this, you need to liberate yourself from all of the limitations and boundaries, all of the fear, threats, and psychological games, all of the walls, doors, and ceilings that others constantly impose on us. Break through to your own personal freedom!

EB / E'
RULER OF THE TRECENA OF PATHWAYS

original artwork, printed here in black & white,
courtesy of Maree Gifkins

EB / E'
The Trecena of Pathways

E
b, or E' in K'iche' Maya, represents the Road, the *Saq B'e* or sacred path that we all travel on our quest for self-fulfillment and realization. This is the path of destiny, the road we travel to develop, discover, and evolve our personal history and future imprinting; it is also the activity and movement of travel, moving us toward our horizon, our goals and aims in life. It is the connection between people, places, dimensions, and worlds. In that vein, Eb represents the stairways between the three worlds of the heavens, the Earth, and *Xib'alb'a* or the underworld. It also symbolizes thanks and gratitude, blessing, and benediction. Eb is the patron of travelers, protector of merchants, and the nagual of all roads and road guides. Eb's animal totems are the thrush and the bobcat. In the Classical Maya tradition, it is associated with the cardinal direction South and the color yellow. In the tradition of modern-day K'iche' Maya, it is West and the color black. Eb is also one of the four Year Bearers, which shape the nature and character of the solar years they are associated with.

On Eb days, the Maya give thanks for the Road of Life that we all travel, and ask for physical and mental well-being and meaningful occupations. This is the most auspicious day in the Tzolk'in to begin a journey of any kind, be it personal, professional, or other: leaving for a trip, groundbreaking for a new house, signing contracts, or starting new business or professional relationships. It is also a great day for communication—especially international communication— to and from friends, loved ones, and/or colleagues living overseas.

Eb is *Saq B'e*, in the material sense the *White Road* that connects Mayan temples and ceremonial centers, and in the spiritual sense the sacred path that propels us forward on the course of self-realization and life fulfillment. This is the realm of the seeker who cannot turn back once she has seen Truth, and despite efforts to forget, is forever changed by the experience. This is the pilgrim who must get lost in order to find himself, who is willing to open his very soul to discovery and exploration so that he may once again enjoy things new and wondrous that children see. And as they wind through life's unceasing turns, the white roads that connect us all to our past and future selves, return, always, to the center of our soul.

The paths we travel evolve and change through experience and time, accelerate to vertiginous speeds and slow to a deep silence, split into myriad strings of existence and fuse again into the thick luminous band that guides our journey. We travel within and through time, passing from one life stage to the next, assimilating the energy of each one into our soul. We travel physically, today more than ever before in the history of our species, and incarnate the stresses of multiple cultures, time zones, and distances. We travel emotionally, our psyche growing and evolving as we meet new people, create new bonds and release those we no longer wish to hold. We travel mentally, some of us forever exploring new horizons in skill, innovation, and knowledge, some of us content with simpler routines and the comforts of home. And we travel spiritually, covering depths and distances much greater than our physical bodies could ever dream of, and dimensions that perhaps only our higher souls are aware of.

Any journey we undertake, whether a vacation overseas, a business trip, a new career, a new relationship, or a spiritual exploration, changes or affects us in some way. The more open we keep heart and mind, the deeper into Truth we see, the more vibrant the colors of the landscapes we explore, the more fascinating the people we meet, the more enriching our experience and enjoyment of life.

The essence of Eb is not so much about traveling on a path as becoming the path yourself. How so? By channeling who you are and what you know, what you inspire and what you receive, through your heart and soul, through your being and your mind, through your actions towards others, as a mighty river might cut through solid rock to carve its way.

We are all wondrously individual, unique, vibrant living beings; and so we will all experience the energies coursing through this trecena in very personal ways. As we should... for there are no two *Saq B'e* alike.

Hun (1) Eb
Jun (1) E'

The essence of Eb is not so much about traveling on a path as becoming the path yourself. How so? By accepting who you are and releasing ego, judgment and comparison. By allowing others to be who they are, without imposition, guilt or obligation. By freeing yourself from false dreams, ambitions and desires. By channeling all that you are and do, through your thoughts, feelings and actions, to a higher, purer intention and resonance.

Ka (2) Ben
Kieb (2) Aj

Even the most nomadic of travelers needs a home. Home is where the heart is, as they say... and on this day ruled by Ben and Ka, it is especially true. Your home is not only a physical place infused with you and your family's essence and memories, but a very sacred place where your soul resides. This is the place you come from, the energy that is you, and will always be, regardless of where you live in the world. Honor your spiritual and physical homes today.

Ox (3) Ix
Oxib' (3) I'x

The Jaguar walks the same jungle paths, day after day, night after night, retracing his footprints with a precision that confounds the best trackers. If you seek to walk the path of Ix and align your footsteps with the ancient vital energy he carries, tread carefully today! For Ix is also the nagual of the seven human sins—pride, ambition, envy, lying, crime, ingratitude, ignorance through laziness—and Ox throws countless dangers, traps and obstacles in your way. Keep your eyes open, heart pure and mind focused, and resist the temptation of an easier path.

Kan (4) Men
Kahib' (4) Tz'ikin

The true direction of a road is best seen from high above. If at any time you feel down or unmotivated, call on Men to take you into the stratosphere of your life, and gaze upon the wondrous path you are traveling, in its full and complete totality. Up here, each day becomes an individual pearl in a long and dazzling string, each with its unique imprint and meaning. Disparage not your individual days for want of appreciation of your life as a whole.

Ho (5) Cib
Job' (5) Ajmaq

The ancient concepts of sin and pleasure, of forgiveness and pardon have always been closely intertwined. One defines the other. Today, the energy of Ho may cause you to make a hasty decision, rush into a situation you may regret later, or speak without concern for the consequences of your words, so think through potential outcomes before you act. Be aware of your personal faults and vices, and how they may impact others in your life. If you can find it within you to forgive yourself, you will open the way to resolve and heal those traits, habits and addictions holding you down.

Uac (6) Caban
Wakib' (6) No'j

Your life is a journey. It is a journey of time, of thoughts and experiences, of emotions and memories. It is a journey you have chosen to undertake, so that you may awaken your soul along the way. Think of your life not in terms of the here and now, not from the point of view of your goals, dreams and desires, but as a string of pearls, an ocean of droplets, a desert of sands, which compose the greater whole. This is what Caban and Uac, walking along Eb, the Road of Life, will help you do: to light awake your mind and your consciousness, in a calm, stable, and centered energetic environment.

Uuc (7) Etznab
Wukub' (7) Tijax

The keen insight of Etznab helps you pierce the many veils we live wrapped up in, and see the way things are, simply and directly. Uuc only intensifies the blinding light of truth, for it enables you to see things from all sides. Today is like having a multidimensional sword of truth to slice your path through the overgrown jungles of others' personal myths, falsehoods and agendas that have been strangling your own psychic freedom and purity all these years— likely without you noticing. As you journey through Eb's trecena, use the sword wisely.

Uaxac (8) Cauac
Wajxaqib' (8) Kawoq

Droplets of sunshine droplets of rain showers of joy currents of pain… this is life in all of its beauty and all of its power; nothing is wrong and nothing is right. Everything simply is. Let go today! Don't analyze, don't plan, do not fear or doubt, just let go and get swept up in this beautiful raindance we call being alive.

May Cauac and Uaxac soak your soul with loving, caring rain, the kind that brings life to fresh-sown fields, radiance to your cheeks, and laughter to your children.

Bolon (9) Ahau
B'elejeb' (9) Ajpu

Bolon pulls the powerful intuitive energies inherent in Ahau to the surface, as if drawing a massive solar flare to the face of the sun. Whatever has been holding hostage your own powers of intuition and innate knowledge, cracks and withers in the blistering power of Ahau's fierce glare. Take advantage of your moment and break free of the chains that have held your natural energy and vitality prisoner, whether psychological, mental, emotional, physical or spiritual.

This is especially important for you if you're a woman, as Bolon carries a distinctly feminine essence.

Lahun (10) Imix
Lajuj (10) Imox

A good day to help a friend or loved one who may be suffering from anxiety, anguish, or some kind of psychological distress, disorder or emotional turmoil, whether chronic or temporary. Much of the profound unhappiness that affects people today stems from the breakdown of our social fabric and values, the critical support structures of society. Lahun helps rebuild bonds and relationships, especially those torn up by Imix's churning currents.

Buluk (11) Ik'
Junlajuj (11) Iq'

Today, Ik' is guided by the undercurrent of Eb and the great force and power of Buluk (Eleven). If you know your path and purpose in life, harness today's powerful energies to propel you forward by a quantum leap. If you are still uncertain, then use the energies to discover it.

Above all, remember that neither Ik' nor Buluk are inherently positive or negative—they are much like the forces of nature: pure power, to be utilized according to intention. So whatever your will or intention, be sure it is the right one.

La Ka (12) Akb'al
Kablajuj (12) Aq'ab'al

Today presents an interesting mix of energies: Akb'al embodies potential and La Ka represents a full accounting of things already lived and done. But because we are in the trecena of Eb, the nagual of all roads, the apparent chasm between potential and realized experience becomes one continuous line rendering the relativity of time immaterial. In other words, you can express and experience all of the collective potential of your life at any moment, but especially so today.

Oxlahun (13) Kan
Oxlajuj (13) K'at

Whether you're working through karma from past lives or generations, or issues and difficulties now present in your life, you typically go through the same cycles of awareness, acceptance, action, resolution, and finally freedom. You may, in fact, find yourself running through several iterations of these cycles on the same issue if it's particularly complicated or challenging... much like the way you wash a shirt several times if it's impossibly soiled. Oxlahun enhances your perception, sharpens your intuition and helps you unravel the knots in your spiritual and psychological bodies so that your work may progress faster and smoother.

Chicchan / Kan
Ruler of the Trecena
of Energy and Evolution

original artwork, printed here in black & white,
courtesy of Maree Gifkins

CHICCHAN / KAN
The Trecena of Energy and Evolution

Associated with the mystical Feathered Serpent, Kukulkan or Quetzalcoatl as the Aztecs called this deity, Chicchan, or Kan in K'iche' Maya, is one of the most powerful day signs in the Tzolk'in. The Regent of the Sky and the Ruler of Time, Chicchan symbolizes the transformation of time, transcendence, peace, spiritual development and human evolution, and represents those predestined for spiritual vocations. Yet it is also the lord of all material things and represents the concepts of work, autonomy, precaution, power, law, intelligence, and justice. As the nagual of education and training, it signifies the power that learning imparts to individuals and communities. Chicchan is also the nagual of the creation of new human life, the transformation of knowledge into wisdom, and embodies a powerful connection with the inner fire, called *koyopa* among the Maya and *kundalini* in Eastern traditions. It activates sexual energy as the essence of *koyopa* and the awe-inspiring strength and power of life itself. Chicchan's animal totem is the serpent. In the Classical Maya tradition, it is associated with the cardinal direction East and the color red. In the tradition of modern-day K'iche' Maya, it is North and the color white.

On Chicchan days, the Maya ask for answers and solutions to all kinds of problems, issues, and necessities. Chicchan helps you develop your inner fire and evolve spiritually. This is a good day to build physical strength, demand that vitality, clarity, and understanding immediately manifest in your life, and to neutralize fear, dread, and anxiety. It is also a powerful day for sexual matters of all kinds, such as asking for a partner, reconciliation between couples, and finding sexual balance.

Perhaps one of the most striking, beautiful, and awe-inspiring visions in the cultural psyche of humankind is the plumed serpent. The serpent has played a profound role in our collective mythology since the earliest times, mesmerizing humanity across geographies and across time—from Egypt and Babylon to Greece and Rome, from Chinese dynasties and Hebrew tribes to Hindu cultures and the many native peoples of the Americas—at once feared and revered as an archetypal symbol of power, sexual energy, and eternal mysteries. The serpent is also frequently associated with the feminine principle, for its mystical essence mirrors the power a woman holds to bear and give life, a power that throughout human history men have tried to control, suppress, and conquer; hence the multitudinous and ambivalent interpretations of the serpent in so many of the world's cultures and beliefs.

Chicchan, the Serpent, embodies deep, instinctive wisdom and intelligence, but also profound, powerful emotion and energy that can cause great upheaval and change. For the Maya, the Feathered Serpent embodies the very energy of life, *koyopa*, energy in its purest and simplest form, that can be neither judged nor denied. This is the energy that guides, that fulfills, that changes, mutates, and evolves all that it touches. This is the energy embodied within the stars of which all things are made, the DNA of existence and consciousness. All of us carry this sacred energy deep within, for that is what we are made of. Yet we spend our lives denying, ignoring, or living in fear of it. You may notice this trend throughout this book... fear, control, denial of potential, denial of freedom. These are the true dark forces—not some imagined threat, politicized evil, or a fabricated, hyper-marketed "disease"—that continue to affront us, within and without, and that we must seek to neutralize if we are to develop and evolve as the spiritual, emotional, and physical human beings that we are.

As so many of the day signs and daily energies in this book suggest, most of the work we need to do is internal. For it's there, deep within the inner fire of our souls that our thoughts are born, our emotions ignite, our dreams take flight and our actions initiate. At least that is where it all *should* begin. Too much of what we think, feel, and do is the result of an external influence, whether it's media, marketing, other people's opinions, societal customs, or established infrastructure and regulation. Give it a try—the next time you react or respond to something or someone, ask yourself if this is truly you or an imprinted message from somewhere or someone else. It's time to get back in touch with ourselves and re-embody the energies that make us who we are, as individuals, as members of society, as creators of our lives, as active elements of the greater universal consciousness.

Hun (1) Chicchan
Jun (1) Kan

Open up your heart and soul and gaze into your own eyes, for therein lie the eternal rhythms of the universe. Never forget you are part of the vast cycles of life, connected and interconnected to all other living things. Denying or ignoring this vital connection alienates you from others, severs your contact with nature, isolates you from essential resources and support networks, and leads to the social ills and destructive patterns so prevalent now on all levels of modern life.

Reconnect, re-embrace, and re-align with your inner fire, your *koyopa*. Let it burn bright once again.

Ka (2) Cimi
Kieb (2) Kame

Perhaps the most painfully poignant dichotomy is that of life and death—there is nothing so vibrant, so ecstatic, so utterly awe-inspiring as life and its infinite array of color, form, and movement; and nothing so inert, so silent, so profoundly permanent as death and its inevitable reach that touches all that lives. Take neither for granted, for they both serve a vital purpose.

Enjoy life and respect death.

Ox (3) Manik'
Oxib' (3) Kej

Walk, don't run, with the energies of today. Ox's disruptive forces threaten to destabilize Manik', the mighty stag, and throw him off his sure-footed gait. And Manik' is, as they say, too big to fall. The power and force inherent in this day sign can wreak a lot of havoc if disrupted or sent down the wrong path. Respect Manik's energy, take your time in learning how to harness its power, and steer it clear of people, situations, and places that may introduce doubt, risk, and uncertainty to your path or intention.

Kan (4) Lamat
Kahib' (4) Q'anil

One of the wisest things you can do is dedicate some time each day to rest, relax and enjoy yourself. Nothing in the extreme is healthy—neither work nor play, and "productivity" or "busy-ness" is not as great a virtue as Western society would have you believe. Ancient civilizations knew that abundance and wealth in life are not obtained by working 90-hour weeks, but by replenishing your mind, spirit and body with a healthy balance of work, play, rest and activity.

Ho (5) Muluc
Job' (5) Toj

Some believe that to get ahead in life, you need to get there—whereever "there" is—as fast as possible, before someone else does. In fact, the opposite is true. To speed up, you need to slow down. The same goes for achieving that elusive work-life balance we are all chasing on a daily basis. It's not about how fast we do it, or how soon. It's all about how deeply we love, how well we treat others, and how much we respect ourselves. Build these pillars into your daily life and everything else will follow naturally.

Uac (6) Oc
Wakib' (6) Tz'i

Oc, the nagual of sexuality, is today set against the energetic background of Chicchan, the Feathered Serpent, which also embodies sexual matters. The combination yields an explosive sexual energy that can quickly overflow into uncontrollable passions were it not for the stability and calming effect of Uac (Six). With this, honor your sexuality as an essential, natural and healthy part of your being, not a sin or vice to be hidden or shamed.

Uuc (7) Chuen
Wukub' (7) B'atz'

When the Monkey dances by the light of the moon, strange things become normal, and the usual turns bizarre. Inevitably, human tendency is to qualify the unusual or the unknown, to label or judge, without forethought or consideration. But today, there is no need—for the energies are playing your music. So relax, enjoy Chuen's irreverent frolicking, and allow your creative juices to flow to their fullest, without judgment, qualification or desire. Explore, play, try out new ways of thinking—and let Uuc guide you as you decide which of these seeds you should plant and grow, and which you should let expire.

Uaxac (8) Eb
Wajxaqib' (8) E'

Today, honor the lifepath that you, or perhaps someone close to you, are traveling, for it is a journey that is as sacred as it is vital. For many Maya, Uaxac represents the weaving of life, of the thread of Time—and there are few more auspicious energy partners for Uaxac than Eb. The double helix formed by Eb's *saq b'e*, the sacred road, and Uaxac's cord of life, illuminates, heals and nurtures your mind, body and soul, and enables you to plug directly into the source of your *koyopa* (the Maya concept of *kundalini*).

Honor your lifepath.

Bolon (9) Ben
B'elejeb' (9) Aj

Bolon in the context of Ben and Chicchan is an extremely powerful force, especially for pregnant women or expectant couples. Whether you are expecting or already have children, honor their spirit and souls today, as their parents and guardians of the most sacred of responsibilities—that of creating life and bringing to this world new human beings, whose experience of life, outlook and journey through life, indeed, whose very future lies partly in your hands. In turn, we are all children ourselves; honor your parents and their ancestors, and the work and sacrifice they made to give us the best of their own lives.

Lahun (10) Ix
Lajuj (10) I'x

For the Jaguar, it's a real challenge to work in a group or to relate closely to others, as he is by nature secretive, mystical... a lone spirit walking through the shadows of the night. If Ix is your day sign, or you have this trait or tendency, use Lahun's energy today to break out of your shell and enrich and strengthen the relationships you have with your family, friends and others in your life you care about. And no worries... this doesn't mean becoming a public figure. You can still maintain your very private personal and inner life.

Buluk (11) Men
Junlajuj (11) Tz'ikin

Its force multiplied by Buluk and its soul sanctified by Chicchan, Men sweeps in the winds of evolution and change on its powerful wings. Forget petty ambitions like fame, riches and power, which are but illusory and can go up in an instant flame. Commune instead with your highest incarnation, the highest expression of your soul. Gain acute clarity of vision and depth of understanding into what stands in the way of fulfilling your true potential, from your past through to your present and into your future. Judge not, but simply accept and heed the insights you receive today, especially if they come in a dream.

La Ka (12) Cib
Kablajuj (12) Ajmaq

Today, stop for a moment and think of the part you play in the evolution of the human species and life itself. Stop the race of thoughts, ambitions, goals, to-do lists, people-to-call lists, the errands and duties and chores. Find some time today to *just be*. Take the time to connect to your family, to the rest of humanity, and to all living things. Think of everything you've done, seen and experienced, recognize and accept all of the influences that have shaped you to be who you are today, and then let it all go.

This, more than anything else, will recharge your soul and spirit.

Oxlahun (13) Caban
Oxlajuj (13) No'j

The sacred *koyopa* energy of Oxlahun (Thirteen) fuses with the intense mental fire of Caban to forge the potential for an explosive breakthrough—a realization, an awakening, an illumination into some aspect of your life, or perhaps the life or situation of someone very close to you.

But don't expect it or try too hard to realize it, for it needs to come on its own, without expectations or insistence. Your mind is an extremely powerful thing, and for these moments of sacred clarity, it needs to be completely free of judgment, ego and desire.

Etznab / Tijax
Ruler of the Trecena of
Truth and Healing

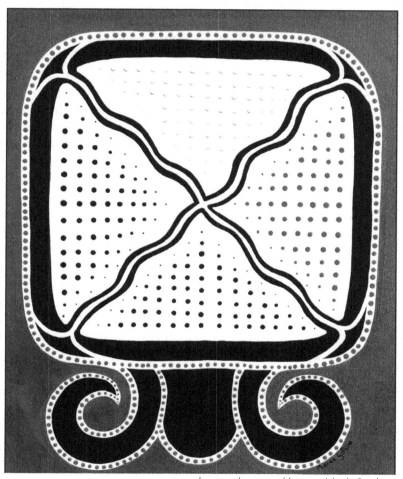

original artwork, printed here in black & white,
courtesy of Maree Gifkins

ETZNAB / TIJAX
The Trecena of Truth and Healing

E tznab, or Tijax in K'iche' Maya, is the day sign of Obsidian, an extremely sharp natural glass formed by volcanic activity that among the Maya is most prized by diviners and warriors. Like obsidian that embodies the forces of nature that forged it, Etznab symbolizes the power of thunder and lightning. Like obsidian, Etznab is sharp yet fragile, difficult to polish and manipulate, and cuts to the core of things with all of the force of integrity. It cuts through not only deception, evil, and negative energies, but also physical illness. For this reason it is an auspicious sign for healers (*curanderas*), surgeons and doctors, for all matters of health and wellness, medicine and curing of disease. Etznab is also known as Flint, especially in the form of a spear or knife. And like a knife, it has a double edge. On the one hand, it represents communication, eloquence, publicity, education, and teaching. On the other, it signifies vengeance, espionage, falsehood, gossip, and quarrels. This duality makes it a very challenging day, for duality generates conflict. True to this aspect of its nature, Etznab is the nagual of suffering and sudden death—in whatever form or meaning. The animal totem of Etznab is the wolf. In the Classical Maya tradition, it is associated with the cardinal direction North and the color white. In the tradition of modern-day K'iche' Maya, it is South and the color yellow.

On Etznab days, the Maya pray for safety from all harm and for the resolution of all conflict. They ask for health not just for themselves and their families, but for their enemies as well, so that all negative energies may dissipate or be abandoned. Etznab days should be used to end negative or harmful relationships, finding balance, purifying our thoughts and actions, and seeing through to the core of things with the aid of minerals and crystals.

In modern Western society we have two sayings: "truth hurts" and "the truth shall set you free." Strange perhaps the link between pain and freedom, yet many of us know it all too well. The history of our race is held together by chains, of the iron and the psychological kind. Like the sharp edge of an obsidian knife, truth can indeed cause pain to those not ready or willing to embrace it, but when utilized with wisdom, integrity, and honor, the initial pain will give way to strength, character, and confidence—and great personal freedom. Truth heals.

We spend a great deal of our lives hiding or obscuring truth: we twist words, we hide evidence, we spread false rumors, we misrepresent actions, situations, and intentions. And yes, some of us outright lie. Our political figures use the art of diplomacy to glaze over unpleasant or even unethical acts to serve their interests; the CEOs of our companies employ legions of executive yes-men (and women) and PR and marketing resources to inflate the perception of success and leadership; and when it comes to personal relationships, the depth of deception goes further than the bottom of the ocean. Why is this? What drives so many of us to subvert the truth and integrity of others as well as ourselves? Perhaps because that is what we have been taught by parents who in turn learned these false songs from their parents. Perhaps because we prefer the easy way to all that we want. Or perhaps because truth, honor, and kindness are toxic to the gods of money, power, and fame that feed on our psyches.

It may also be because one person's truth is not that of another. Even our own truth one day may not be the same truth the next. The reality in which we live is relative not only to itself, but also to that of others—if we so allow it. Therein lies the knot at the center of the web: what is our personal truth?

The challenge this trecena is to stand before the mirror of your soul unclad and unfettered by fear, uncertainty, weakness or falsehood of any kind. Etznab, sharp black Obsidian, cuts through the slippery veils we live wrapped up in, through the layers of misguided ambitions, fear, and greed that our social and media conditioning hypnotizes us with, through the fog that obscures the clarity and potential of our lives. Break through this screen of smoke and fog spun over your soul over an entire lifetime, and recognize who you truly are. When you do, everything in your life becomes clear, and the path you walk gains direction and purpose. And all else follows suit: your physical, mental, and emotional health.

There is no journey like the search for personal truth.

Hun (1) Etznab
Jun (1) Tijax

Stand before the mirror of your soul, unclad and unfettered. Bleed out from your psychic body the poisons of fear, uncertainty, weakness and falsehood. Have the courage to look directly into your heart, body and mind, without prejudice and without judgment, but with full acceptance and recognition of that which needs work or improvement. Rejoice in that which you have made already strong and pure, and commit to new and future steps toward full and complete healing.

Ka (2) Cauac
Kieb (2) Kawoq

A rainstorm can bring the gift of fertile soils to parched fields or it can destroy entire cities. It doesn't take much for a life-giving rain to turn into a devastating typhoon. Because there is such a fine line between the two extremes of the power of Cauac, you'll need to make sure that you direct the ever-present potential for drama and upheaval in this day sign toward the positive things that you desire. And to do so, you need to see very, very far down the road you're traveling—use the very same power of Cauac to cleanse the mirror of Etznab, the ruler of this trecena, so that you may see a clearer, deeper, purer truth.

Ox (3) Ahau
Oxib' (3) Ajpu

In any conflict or challenge, the most debilitating force comes in the form of the uncertain, the untested and the unknown. Today, Ox will present you with your opponent, whether it be human or animal, situational or physical, mental or psychological. If you're already dealing with something or someone, Ox may either triple that struggle or endow you with three times the strength and resolve. No matter how difficult your specific situation, however, Ahau rules the day to empower you with brilliant intuition and leadership, sharpen your resolve still further with Etznab's sword of truth, and strengthen the willpower and confidence you need to emerge victorious.

Kan (4) Imix
Kahib' (4) Imox

Kan completes Imix. Four is the number of dimensions in which we experience physical reality—so if there is anything destabilizing you, your mental state or any aspect of your life, use Kan's wholesome energy to set things right again. Likewise, if world events, the behavior of friends or loved ones, or circumstances outside of your control are making you feel helpless, frustrated or about to lose your mind, set your feet on Kan's rock-solid foundation and call on Imix to present some alternate solutions to what seem like impossible challenges.

Ho (5) Ik'
Job' (5) Iq'

Careful today about rushing headfirst into something you have not quite thought through, especially if it involves telling someone the truth they may not be ready to hear. Ik' is a cleansing, purifying force, but it can also strip you and your relationships of the protective coat of diplomacy, courtesy, and subtlety. So weigh your words with care and compassion, and anticipate their impact and effect before you speak.

Uac (6) Akb'al
Wakib' (6) Aq'ab'al

Sometimes we want to have potential that we simply don't. Be honest with yourself—you must learn to tell the difference between recognizing true, natural potential and wanting to be someone or wishing for a specific talent or trait. Otherwise you may end up spending a lifetime chasing an impossible dream. Remember that the path of least resistance is usually the path that was made for you.

Uuc (7) Kan
Wukub' (7) K'at

In order to plant new seeds, you've got to turn over the soil. This means tying up loose strings, closing out open issues, ending toxic relationships. Use Uuc's powerful closing or "end" energies to clear your field, and Kan's fertile essence to sow fresh new realities into your life, or that of your loved ones. You may not be able to clear all of the challenges and issues in your life on this one day—and no one would expect you to! Do a little on each Uuc day, but do it well, and you shall progress steadily.

Uaxac (8) Chicchan
Wajxaqib' (8) Kan

Your soul is an ever-evolving energy cycling through the stages of life, immortal, infinite, omnipotent. In its purest state, your essence easily transcends the heavy, binding chains that those who thrive on fear, falsehood, control, ignorance, malice, and greed impose on those who thrive on love, truth, freedom, knowledge, compassion, and generosity. Become aware of the forces seeking to diminish your *koyopa*, your inner fire, make your peace with them—and deny them their power.

Bolon (9) Cimi
B'elejeb' (9) Kame

A day thoroughly infused with vibrant, life-giving feminine energies. The feminine embodies the divine power to create life, to nurture transformation, to drive evolution. If you are pregnant, honor the sacred new life you carry within your womb—as is ideal to do on every Bolon day. If you are not, honor the sacred potential to give life—on so many levels and in so many ways—that you embody. And if you're not female, honor the feminine in your soul and in your life, however it chooses to manifest!

Lahun (10) Manik'
Lajuj (10) Kej

Channel the authority and respect that you command within your circles, not for the fulfillment of the ego but for the betterment of those around you—regardless of what they may think of you. They may not share the depth or breadth of your vision or insight, and may resist you at first. Nor does it matter if your family or circle of friends is small, or has no apparent significant influence on society. Remember the power of one only needs a few iterations to expand to a massive volume of energy.

If you can open the eyes of one, you free a generation.

Buluk (11) Lamat
Junlajuj (11) Q'anil

There is tremendous force in today's energies that you will need to harness before they steamroll you. Because Buluk (Eleven) is a neutral number, its energy can cause the power of Lamat's abundance and growth to yield results or effects that you may or may not desire—much like that of a great tidal wave or flood: the waters can bring another year of rich harvests or wreak destruction across the land. Fortunately, Lamat does tend to be very positive, so as long as you are aware and confident in what you are asking for or acting on, you should expect to achieve it on a much grander scale or level than usual.

La Ka (12) Muluc
Kablajuj (12) Toj

On either side of harmony, there is discord and cacophony. On either side of balance, there is disequilibrium and instability. As you walk Etznab's knife edge today, reflect upon your life past, present, and future: the experiences you've had and the lessons you've learned, where you are now, and your dreams and goals still ahead. Accept responsibility for decisions you've made and for the things you have caused to manifest, acknowledge your karmic debt, and let Muluc guide you toward the kind of harmony, balance and inner peace you can only gain once you've learned to walk that higher middle path.

Oxlahun (13) Oc
Oxlajuj (13) Tz'i

Eastern medicine considers that the patient is just as, if not more, responsible for his or her own health. This means having not only the knowledge but the authority to decide how best to heal your body and maintain strong, vibrant health long into the future. Today, harness the psychic energy of Oxlahun to tune into your body and go straight to the core of whatever ails you or needs attention now. Listen to the advice of your doctors and health professionals, especially those in holistic or Eastern medicine, but do your research and make the final decision yourself.

Chuen / B'atz'
Ruler of the Trecena of Creativity

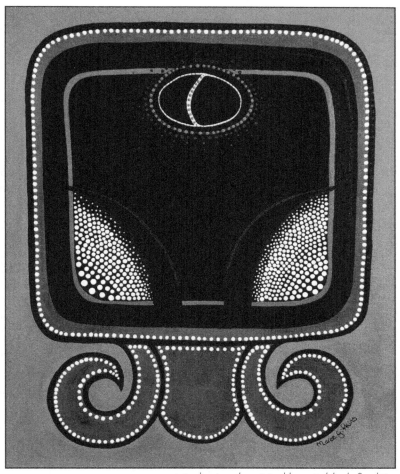

*original artwork, printed here in black & white,
courtesy of Maree Gifkins*

CHUEN / B'ATZ'
The Trecena of Creativity

Master of all the Arts, Chuen, or B'atz' in K'iche' Maya, is the weaver of the thread of life and the cords of time. For the Maya, history is woven with the thread of time just as clothing is sewn from the fibers of plants. Chuen symbolizes evolution, movement, motion, and development; initiation, affirmation, and favorable divination readings; intelligence and wisdom; and especially marriage and pregnancy—the *tz'ite* representing the Mayan priests, the *ajq'ijab'*, contains 260 seeds, which symbolize the nine months of pregnancy. Chuen is the nagual of the arts, artists, and the art of weaving, and as such, represents all concepts and elements of life related to art and weaving, from time itself—called by the Maya "the thread of life"—to the life-connecting umbilical cord. Not surprisingly, Chuen is often referred to as "Monkey," for monkeys were the mythic patrons of the arts in ancient Mayan lore. The monkey is, in fact, Chuen's animal totem. In the Classical Maya tradition, it is associated with the cardinal direction West and the color black. In the tradition of modern-day K'iche' Maya, it is East and the color red.

On Chuen days, the Maya express their intention to freely receive all that they have requested from the universe, and to be able to unravel or resolve any matter or issue, especially family problems. Chuen days are extremely auspicious for all artistic works and endeavors; in fact, it is a powerful day to begin any project. And it is the best day in the Tzolk'in to ask for a partner or to be married.

In Maya culture, you dance around the fire of a sacred ceremony thirteen times from right to left, unwinding the spool of time, and then thirteen times again in the opposite direction, so that you may wind it back up again. It is said that the Creators threw a spool of thread to the end of the universe, which of course unraveled, then wound it up and tossed it back again. Accordingly, the upcoming thirteen days embody a magical period of creativity, art, music, dance, and play. This is the time to slip out of your rigid professional persona, leave that business suit and tie in the closet, and let the real, creative you thrive, no matter who you are, where you come from, or what work you do.

Chuen can help you transform your life from a dull cycle of the mundane daily tasks of modern existence to one of an endlessly vibrant, exuberant dance of experiences. I know of many such transformations: a Wall Street investment broker who quit his job to dedicate his life to photography; a Washington DC accountant who shed his corporate skin to be the painter he always knew he was; a PR executive who started an environmental video production company. You no doubt know many others. Who says you need to stay where you are, or keep going to that soul-killing job? What is your purpose: make money, attain power or fame, dedicate yourself to your children, drive your talents to their peak, protect our natural world, leave a lasting legacy to future generations…? Whatever your purpose may be, if you're not waking up each and every day in love with life and eager to start the day, you're not fulfilling your soul.

But first, get in tune with your personal time. Use Chuen days to do this. Pay attention to patterns, cycles in your life that seem to repeat, circumstances that keep taking you to certain places or certain people, things that keep happening despite all of your efforts to the contrary. This will illuminate your unique, individual life history, the pattern woven by your personal time; only then can you start to weave a different pattern which can lead to a richer, more creative lifepath.

As you discover your personal time, explore without *looking* for anything specific—you need to keep ego out of the process. Most importantly, *do not compare*. To repeat, do not compare yourself to others, celebrities you see in glossy magazines, wealthy executives, or even your family or neighbors. You are you.

As with any creative or magical power, you need to respect and honor Chuen, and guide it to help you as you would any wild untamed force of nature. Lose sense of what you're doing and it will snap into chaos.

Do you have the courage to be who you are?

Hun (1) Chuen
Jun (1) B'atz'

Great day to break open the cans of creative paint you've been storing away in your subconscious, and let the colors fly.   Imagination, inspiration, and innovation rule the day, unbridled, untamed, and unfiltered. So don't hold back, go a little wild! Splatter the canvas of your day with everything you've got and see what happens. If your life is too structured or you don't know where to start, start by taking plenty of time alone for you today—you'll be amazed how quickly your natural ability to imagine resurfaces. All you need is to be with you.

Ka (2) Eb
Kieb (2) E'

Sooner or later, all paths come to a crossroads. Which way now? Ka presents you with a choice between two options at this point of your life's journey—consider them carefully, for once you turn onto a certain route, the farther along you travel, the more difficult it is to return. But tarry not too long in choosing, either, for indecision can lead to stagnation... and Ka won't keep the doors open forever.

Ox (3) Ben
Oxib' (3) Aj

You may experience some level of uncertainty or challenge on the home front today, or possibly with your children, or parents, as the case may be. Rather than address the issue from an authoritarian standpoint—especially if you're the parent—try a little playfulness, a little creativity to approach it from a different angle. It may seem risky, but without risk there is little discovery. Let Ben, buoyed by Chuen's frisky nature, guide you to some surprising answers.

Kan (4) Ix
Kahib' (4) I'x

Awaken the natural artist and creator within you, and walk with Ix, the Jaguar, to the four corners of your psyche—the North, South, East and West of your soul—to reaquaint yourself with your essence, your creativity, your skills and talents so that you may thrive once again as a complete human being rather than the box or label modern society wants you to be.

Reconnect with your source.

Ho (5) Men
Job' (5) Tz'ikin

A good day to mix all those ambitions and dreams with a little creative magic. Men, the Eagle, brings you a far greater perspective to see it all from 36,000 feet. So leave your Excel spreadsheets and to-do lists behind, and come along for a heady ride into the realm of inspiration and creativity. Here, no limitations obscure your vision, no obstacles hinder your flight. Just raw, unrefined dreams and possibilities.

No good dreaming big if you don't have any imagination!

Uac (6) Cib
Wakib' (6) Ajmaq

At first glance, Uac may appear to contradict the very essence of Cib: its practical, down-to-earth focus on the here and now, contrasted with the ancestral wisdom and old soul energy that Cib carries. In fact, few energies are more compatible—the most practically applicable knowledge and insights generally come from the elders, the ancestors, those who precede us and who have paved the way. We learn from their experience, their mistakes, their forays into uncharted territory.

Honor the paths paved by your ancestors.

Uuc (7) Caban
Wukub' (7) No'j

Caban is all about intellect, logic and rational thinking. Deep introspection rules the day, but since this is Chuen's trecena, you might want to crack that door open a bit and let in some fresh air. Think thoughts you don't usually dare.

But, as with all things, do think twice before turning them to action. That's the danger of Seven—as the middle number of the thirteen, it represents complete neutrality, and can go either way. Besides, we don't want a line of people at our door complaining that we've stirred up a whole town.

Uaxac (8) Etznab
Wajxaqib' (8) Tijax

See the world the way children do... pure reflections of naked truth, innocence born of the summer wind, laughter, play and imagination running wilder than horses across vast spring meadows... children will teach you how to see the world the way it really is, not the way we adults have made it out to be. If you want to heal all the pain accumulated over a lifetime and shed all the burdens modern life loads onto our shoulders, then remember how to laugh for no reason, roll around on the grass, stare at the sky for hours, and forget how to feel guilt, shame, envy, ambition, and malice.

They say we've lost the child in us... we say it's still there, giggling!

Bolon (9) Cauac
B'elejeb' (9) Kawoq

Every so often, the day sign and number of a given day complement each other so well and so completely that they become one vivid, vibrant energy. Today is such a day. Cauac and Bolon celebrate the Divine Feminine and its sacred power to give life, channel the forces of nature, and heal the mind, body and soul. Whether you're a woman or a man, celebrate with Cauac and Bolon today, pay respect to the divine feminine that thrives in all human beings and all living things. And if you are a woman, express the highest respect for your innate power to give life; do not ever take it for granted. Treat all children, yours and those of others, with great honor, respect and dignity, for they are the purest incarnations of human potential.

Lahun (10) Ahau
Lajuj (10) Ajpu

You can't be a leader if you have no one to lead. You can't resolve interpersonal issues if you alienate those you need to work with. And you certainly cannot win if there's no one to compete with. Lahun takes Ahau by the hand and brings you right back into the circle of relationships influencing your life right now—whether you're ready or not—because this is the time to work together.

You should have fun doing it, too—this trecena, you're not allowed to be a sourpuss; Chuen makes sure of that! No matter how hard you try to keep a tight lip, giggle energies are in the air, and they're infectious. So relax and go with it. Not everything needs to be a struggle in life.

Buluk (11) Imix
Junlajuj (11) Imox

Ever wonder what it must feel like to be inside a fireworks display? Buluk's supercharged energy ignites Imix's volatile essence into a dazzling display of alternate realities; Chuen, the ruler of this trecena, adds color for a little variety. So what do you do besides watch in stupefied awe? Above all, don't forget you're the one holding the reigns. Pay particular attention to your dreams this morning and tonight, and firmly steer Buluk's and Imix's intensity toward a well-defined horizon.

La Ka (12) Ik'
Kablajuj (12) Iq'

La Ka (Twelve) days are for reflecting on the totality of our life experiences, actions and influences. Today, apply the healing currents of Ik' to sift through and blow away all negative and harmful energies, thoughts and emotions. Today, you can choose the kind of Wind to guide you on your lifepath: a soft gentle breeze to slow down, rest and relax a stressful period; a fierce gale to sweep away pain, anger or suffering; a tropical wind to bring new seeds of potential and creativity to the garden of your soul.

Oxlahun (13) Akb'al
Oxlajuj (13) Aq'ab'al

Oxlahun Akb'al is one of the most pregnant days in the Tzolk'in...
Oxlahun twists the sacred *koyopa* energy into a silken rope that
intertwines its acute intuitive and psychic sensibilities with Akb'al's
thick velvet potential as it enriches and grows through the night into
the dawn of its own awakening. Relax into the night, into its deep
quiet depths where all potential sleeps, where no desire, no stress
can penetrate, where all is in blissful content for simply being.

Kan / K'at
Ruler of the Trecena of
Freedom and Fertility

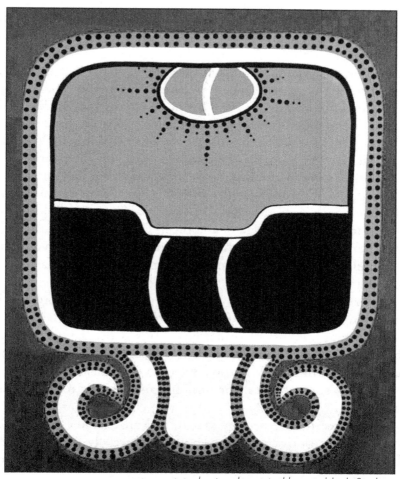

original artwork, printed here in black & white,
courtesy of Maree Gifkins

KAN / K'AT
The Trecena of Freedom and Fertility

The symbol of the sacred Ceiba tree, Kan, or K'at in K'iche' Maya, represents the magic of germination and growth, in the form of new offspring, new crops, and the expansion of future generations. At times called Seed, Kan is considered by some Maya to control the sexual force in the body, and as such, it embodies the power of gender. Within its vast body of meaning, it also signifies the Net, in all of the diversity of senses of the word: a fisherman's net, a woven net for fruits or vegetables, a network, a spider's web; in addition, it is the patron of storerooms and pantries and refers to the gathering of resources; and finally, it carries the concepts of captivity, punishment, social traps, and lawsuits. Kan is the nagual of fire, namely that which keeps a home running, and of prisons both visible and invisible, material and intangible. Kan's animal totems are the alligator and the lizard. In the Classical Maya tradition, it is associated with the cardinal direction South and the color yellow. In the tradition of modern-day K'iche' Maya, it is West and the color black.

On Kan days, the Maya pray for abundance and express their intention to understand, or to seek to understand, their fellow human beings, events or situtations. This is the day to ask that those imprisoned in some way, be freed, and for the tangling and untangling of things. It is also a good day for healing ceremonies and practices, especially if the healing to be done is psychological in nature.

This trecena is especially sacred, as Kan embodies the power to give life and drive evolution, but also especially dangerous, for this potent day sign harbors powerful passions in all aspects of creativity and fertility—from sexual prowess to creative genius to the generation of wealth—that, if left unguided or aligned with the right path, can cause wanton waste, sensual abandon, or excessive indulgence. Like the elemental forces of Nature that rage across the planet in their full power, potency, and diversity of form—water as rain, rivers, and oceans, air as winds, breezes, and hurricanes—Kan makes no value judgments and takes no moral stances. It simply is. The key to allowing the fertile energies of the Kan trecena into your soul, and guiding their power along the path of right intention, is respect. Respect the sanctity of your life, of your own talent, imagination, and capacity for creativity, fertility, abundance. Don't belittle yourself or your abilities, but be realistic in terms of which talents you do indeed possess and where to best channel your creative energies.

In modern human society, the more fertile or resource-rich you are, whether you are a person, another living species, a company, a country, or a natural resource, the more valued, the more desired, the more envied—and the more threatening you are considered, and therefore the more sought after, whether the intention is to control, to exploit, or to own you. Ironically, it is those entities and those interests with the most political and economic power that seek to possess and control, rather than to empower or to express and bestow gratitude, admiration, love, or respect. These entities and individuals rely on fear to keep everyone else—those of us who would prefer to live empowered and free of toxic emotions—under control. That's the imprisonment that Kan represents, the entanglement of the vast personal and global Net that we all need to break so that we can be free of the fear, the competition, the ego, the greed, and other toxic qualities that our various social systems and customs inject us with since the day we are born.

The world we live in is built on power, productivity and money, which are but the technical structures that are supposed to serve the generation of true wealth—that of the mind, body and soul—yet which have taken over the psyche of our society and are now reigning as the ultimate purpose in life. Many are already categorically rejecting this paradigm, and I encourage all of you to rediscover and harness the creative powers you hold deep within your soul. Nature herself expresses her fertility and creativity every breath of every day, blossoming new forms of life, nurturing the tiniest and supporting the biggest, painting vibrant colors across her skies, forests, and seas, unleashing awe-inspiring storms, winds, and earthquakes, yet balancing all of her forces with eternal patience, instinct, and the wisdom of millennia.

You too are a force of Nature. Live your life accordingly.

Hun (1) Kan
Jun (1) K'at

When you cause something to manifest, you carry a responsibility for it. Accept it not as a burden, but as a joy—for the act of creation, of bringing an idea, a concept, or a new living being to life is one of the most awe-inspiring and humbling events any of us will ever experience. Today, with Hun's support, Kan empowers not only the germination of new seeds and the birth of new life, but the release of vital energies heretofore imprisoned, of possibilities frozen in time, or ideas tangled up in the net of inability, lack of resources, or wrong timing. Free your mind and the world is yours.

Ka (2) Chicchan
Kieb (2) Kan

Remember that you hold within you the power to create or to destroy, to evolve or to regress, to connect or disconnect, to see or to ignore. Such is the dichotomy and duality of life and our experience on this earth; our challenge is to free ourselves of all our prisons, internal and external, so that we may make the right decisions and wield this power wisely and justly.

The choice is always yours, no matter how helpless you may feel, no matter how others may try to control you. The choice is always yours.

Ox (3) Cimi
Oxib' (3) Kame

Sometimes, those things in life that most of us would normally avoid, like doubt, risk and uncertainty, turn out to be blessings in disguise. Cimi has the power to kill the negative energies of Ox and cause them to be reborn in a more positive embodiment: doubt can blossom into confidence, risk can turn into opportunity, uncertainty can become wisdom, and obstruction can lead to guidance.

Harness the profound power of Cimi to conquer the obstacles in your life and turn them into pillars of empowerment.

Kan (4) Manik'
Kahib' (4) Kej

To wield real power and authority, you need to be balanced. If you come from a place of misintention, greed, ego, self-interest, vengeance or malice, and you do attain influence and power, rest assured it won't last. Sooner or later cracks in your karma will rent asunder your false fortress. Lasting, sustainable personal power stands firmly on the four pillars of respect, ethics, humility, and leadership. Kan, the number 4, underpins the four powerful legs of Manik' the stag—balance your purpose and intention, and establish your force forever.

Ho (5) Lamat
Job' (5) Q'anil

Today packs a double hit of abundance and fertility. Lamat, nestled in the warm nurturing embrace of Kan and crowned with the precocious tendencies of Ho, drenches you with a sunlit waterfall of creative energy. Whatever you desire that requires fertility and abundance, be it of a spiritual, emotional, psychological, physical, biological or material nature, ask for and be ready to receive it today. Above all, enjoy it, without fear, guilt or shame!

Uac (6) Muluc
Wakib' (6) Toj

If it's difficult achieving balance in your own personal life, accomplishing it within an entire family can seem altogether impossible! But today, Uac and Muluc race to the rescue of the weary parent or head of household with energies that support the vitality and stability of the family, on the part of Uac, and that promote internal harmony and peace, on the part of Muluc. This doesn't mean the balance you seek will somehow magically happen. You still have to do the work—but you've got two powerful energies supporting you.

Uuc (7) Oc
Wukub' (7) Tz'i

Uuc represents the epicenter, the most neutral point of anything—in particular the center of the laws of human beings and of life itself. Today, release your psyche and soul from karmic prisons built by generations of false authority, rules and obligations. Put an end to these "laws" that you have agreed to be subject to all of your life, and enable your own rightful authority to grow and thrive. Just be warned—the old energies will kick and scream, and attempt to pull you back with guilt and threats, but you must persevere and claim your innate rights as a free, independent, dignified human being and member of society.

Uaxac (8) Chuen
Wajxaqib' (8) B'atz'

For the K'iche' Maya, Wajxaqib' B'atz' (Uaxac Chuen) is the first day of the sacred Tzolk'in calendar, and marks a period of festivities and celebrations. Why it begins on an Eight day is unknown, but what is certain is that this is an extremely powerful and propitious day—it is one of those days in the Tzolk'in when the energies of the day sign and the number mirror each other perfectly. Uaxac and Chuen both embody the weaving of life, the thread of time, and the sacred energy of birth. This makes today a blessed day for such sacred rites as weddings, engagements, anniversaries, baby announcements, and other events marking the union of two people or the birth of a new life.

Bolon (9) Eb
B'elejeb' (9) E'

Regardless of race, religion or nationality, we all have a powerful, innate instinct to mark in ritual the commencement of important life journeys—births and birthdays, graduations, weddings and anniversaries, plantings and harvests, and so on. Today, Eb and Bolon join their hands in a marriage of energies to rain blessings and sacred well wishes upon those journeys, whichever you may be celebrating.

Lahun (10) Ben
Lajuj (10) Aj

Be the shining guiding light in your family and home today. You have the skills and personal qualities you need to negotiate conflict, tension and disagreement and bring your most intimate circles together in harmony. The challenge is to learn to wield your personal or domestic authority in a compassionate and dignified manner, while remaining flexible, non judgmental and keeping the door open to the organic, unpredictable nature of family dynamics.

Buluk (11) Ix
Junlajuj (11) I'x

Darker than the night, footsteps more silent than the breath of the moon, the Jaguar steals through the spaces between imagination and knowledge, its piercing vision guiding you away from stale repetitions of worn-out ideas and toward fresh new inspiration, variations on your own evolutionary themes. If you can focus Buluk's tremendous force and align it with the path of the Jaguar, you will refresh your source and your internal power and break any barrier still trying to hold you back—whether it's pride, ego, envy, falsehood, ingratitude, ignorance or laziness.

La Ka (12) Men
Kablajuj (12) Tz'ikin

The seed you carry deep inside can easily be swept up by Men, the Eagle, and carried high up into the sky. This is the seed that contains all of your past, present and future, the totality of your life packed into a shell. Who knows where the great bird's talons will drop it, so that it may germinate and grow into a new embodiment of you. How it happens is up to you: you can guide Men with your intention and goals, or let the seed fall where it may.

Oxlahun (13) Cib
Oxlajuj (13) Ajmaq

An incredibly powerful day, charged with Cib's innate connection to ancestral and evolutionary lines; Oxlahun's ability to enhance and sharpen perception and intuition, and access other dimensions of reality; and the undercurrent of Kan's trecena which supports nurturing, healing and release from prisons both visible and invisible.

If you seek to heal pain and suffering passed down through your family lines, to liberate yourself from fear, oppression and control, or fulfill unrealized potential, today gives you a powerful blend of energies to call upon.

MAYAN CALENDAR TABLES

To help you follow along with the 260 Energies of the Day, we have put together a listing of Gregorian and Mayan (Tzolk'in) dates for the beginning of each trecena for the Gregorian years 2000 through 2020. You can use these tables to find any Mayan Calendar date within this period. If you'd like to calculate your Mayan birth sign or any other Mayan date that occurs outside of this period, refer to the Tzolk'in calculator mentioned on page 11 of this book, or any other reliable calculator.

To find the Mayan Calendar date for the Gregorian date of May 20, 2012, for example, find the year 2012 (page 251) in the Calendar Tables. You will note that the trecena that begins before that date is 1 Cib (May 11) and the trecena that begins after that date is 1 Muluc (May 24). Using the Calendar Board on the next page, if you find the day 1 Cib and assign it the value of May 11, you only need to follow the column in the Calendar Board down the right number of days to arrive at May 20:

May 11 = 1 Cib
May 12 = 2 Caban
May 13 = 3 Etznab
May 14 = 4 Cauac
May 15 = 5 Ahau
May 16 = 6 Imix
May 17 = 7 Ik'
May 18 = 8 Akb'al
May 19 = 9 Kan
May 20 = 10 Chicchan

Or you can count *up* the column (backwards in Tzolk'in time), whichever is closer/easier. Be sure to keep leap years in mind (these are marked by an asterisk in the Calendar Tables).

Also listed in the tables, in **bold font**, are the Mayan New Year's days for each year, along with the name of the year—for example, the Mayan New Year in 2012 takes place on February 22 and is called 13 Caban (the Mayan date of February 22).

THE CALENDAR BOARD

Chuen / B'atz'	8	2	9	3	10	4	11	5	12	6	13	7	1
Eb / E'	9	3	10	4	11	5	12	6	13	7	1	8	2
Ben / Aj	10	4	11	5	12	6	13	7	1	8	2	9	3
Ix / I'x	11	5	12	6	13	7	1	8	2	9	3	10	4
Men / Tz'Ik'in	12	6	13	7	1	8	2	9	3	10	4	11	5
Cib / Ajmaq	13	7	1	8	2	9	3	10	4	11	5	12	6
Caban / No'j	1	8	2	9	3	10	4	11	5	12	6	13	7
Etznab / Tijax	2	9	3	10	4	11	5	12	6	13	7	1	8
Cauac / Kawoq	3	10	4	11	5	12	6	13	7	1	8	2	9
Ahau / Ajpu	4	11	5	12	6	13	7	1	8	2	9	3	10
Imix / Imox	5	12	6	13	7	1	8	2	9	3	10	4	11
Ik' / Iq'	6	13	7	1	8	2	9	3	10	4	11	5	12
Akb'al/Aq'ab'al	7	1	8	2	9	3	10	4	11	5	12	6	13
Kan / K'at	8	2	9	3	10	4	11	5	12	6	13	7	1
Chicchan / Kan	9	3	10	4	11	5	12	6	13	7	1	8	2
Cimi / Kame	10	4	11	5	12	6	13	7	1	8	2	9	3
Manik' / Kej	11	5	12	6	13	7	1	8	2	9	3	10	4
Lamat / Q'anil	12	6	13	7	1	8	2	9	3	10	4	11	5
Muluc / Toj	13	7	1	8	2	9	3	10	4	11	5	12	6
Oc / Tz'i	1	8	2	9	3	10	4	11	5	12	6	13	7

GREGORIAN DATE	MAYAN DATE	GREGORIAN DATE	MAYAN DATE
*2000		**2001**	
Jan 4	1 Chicchan	Jan 2	1 Muluc
Jan 17	1 Etznab	Jan 15	1 Ik'
Jan 30	1 Chuen	Jan 28	1 Men
Feb 12	1 Kan	Feb 10	1 Lamat
Feb 25	1 Caban	Feb 23	1 Imix
Feb 25–Mayan Year 1 Caban		**Feb 24–Mayan Year 2 Ik'**	
Mar 9	1 Oc	Mar 8	1 Ix
Mar 22	1 Akb'al	Mar 21	1 Manik'
Apr 4	1 Cib	Apr 3	1 Ahau
Apr 17	1 Muluc	Apr 16	1 Ben
Apr 30	1 Ik'	Apr 29	1 Cimi
May 13	1 Men	May 12	1 Cauac
May 26	1 Lamat	May 25	1 Eb
Jun 8	1 Imix	Jun 7	1 Chicchan
Jun 21	1 Ix	Jun 20	1 Etznab
Jul 4	1 Manik'	Jul 3	1 Chuen
Jul 17	1 Ahau	Jul 16	1 Kan
Jul 30	1 Ben	Jul 29	1 Caban
Aug 12	1 Cimi	Aug 11	1 Oc
Aug 25	1 Cauac	Aug 25	1 Akb'al
Sep 7	1 Eb	Sep 6	1 Cib
Sep 20	1 Chicchan	Sep 19	1 Muluc
Oct 3	1 Etznab	Oct 2	1 Ik'
Oct 16	1 Chuen	Oct 15	1 Men
Oct 29	1 Kan	Oct 28	1 Lamat
Nov 11	1 Caban	Nov 10	1 Imix
Nov 24	1 Oc	Nov 23	1 Ix
Dec 7	1 Akb'al	Dec 6	1 Manik'
Dec 20	1 Cib	Dec 19	1 Ahau

GREGORIAN DATE	MAYAN DATE	GREGORIAN DATE	MAYAN DATE
2002		**2003**	
Jan 1	1 Ben	Jan 13	1 Oc
Jan 14	1 Cimi	Jan 26	1 Akb'al
Jan 27	1 Cauac	Feb 8	1 Cib
Feb 9	1 Eb	Feb 21	1 Muluc
Feb 22	1 Chicchan	**Feb 24–Mayan Year 4 Eb**	
Feb 24–Mayan Year 3 Manik'		Mar 6	1 Ik'
Mar 7	1 Etznab	Mar 19	1 Men
Mar 20	1 Chuen	Apr 1	1 Lamat
Apr 2	1 Kan	Apr 14	1 Imix
Apr 15	1 Caban	Apr 27	1 Ix
Apr 28	1 Oc	May 10	1 Manik'
May 11	1 Akb'al	May 23	1 Ahau
May 24	1 Cib	Jun 5	1 Ben
Jun 6	1 Muluc	Jun 18	1 Cimi
Jun 19	1 Ik'	Jul 1	1 Cauac
Jul 2	1 Men	Jul 14	1 Eb
Jul 15	1 Lamat	Jul 27	1 Chicchan
Jul 28	1 Imix	Aug 9	1 Etznab
Aug 10	1 Ix	Aug 22	1 Chuen
Aug 23	1 Manik'	Sep 4	1 Kan
Sep 5	1 Ahau	Sep 17	1 Caban
Sep 18	1 Ben	Sep 30	1 Oc
Oct 1	1 Cimi	Oct 13	1 Akb'al
Oct 14	1 Cauac	Oct 26	1 Cib
Oct 27	1 Eb	Nov 8	1 Muluc
Nov 9	1 Chicchan	Nov 21	1 Ik'
Nov 22	1 Etznab	Dec 4	1 Men
Dec 5	1 Chuen	Dec 17	1 Lamat
Dec 18	1 Kan	Dec 30	1 Imix
Dec 31	1 Caban		

GREGORIAN DATE	MAYAN DATE	GREGORIAN DATE	MAYAN DATE
*2004		**2005**	
Jan 12	1 Ix	Jan 10	1 Etznab
Jan 25	1 Manik'	Jan 23	1 Chuen
Feb 7	1 Ahau	Feb 5	1 Kan
Feb 20	1 Ben	Feb 18	1 Caban
Feb 24–Mayan Year 5 Caban		**Feb 23–Mayan Year 6 Ik'**	
Mar 4	1 Cimi	Mar 3	1 Oc
Mar 17	1 Cauac	Mar 16	1 Akb'al
Mar 30	1 Eb	Mar 29	1 Cib
Apr 12	1 Chicchan	Apr 11	1 Muluc
Apr 25	1 Etznab	Apr 24	1 Ik'
May 8	1 Chuen	May 7	1 Men
May 21	1 Kan	May 20	1 Lamat
Jun 3	1 Caban	Jun 2	1 Imix
Jun 16	1 Oc	Jun 15	1 Ix
Jun 29	1 Akb'al	Jun 28	1 Manik'
Jul 12	1 Cib	Jul 11	1 Ahau
Jul 25	1 Muluc	Jul 24	1 Ben
Aug 7	1 Ik'	Aug 6	1 Cimi
Aug 20	1 Men	Aug 19	1 Cauac
Sep 2	1 Lamat	Sep 1	1 Eb
Sep 15	1 Imix	Sep 14	1 Chicchan
Sep 28	1 Ix	Sep 27	1 Etznab
Oct 11	1 Manik'	Oct 10	1 Chuen
Oct 24	1 Ahau	Oct 23	1 Kan
Nov 6	1 Ben	Nov 5	1 Caban
Nov 19	1 Cimi	Nov 18	1 Oc
Dec 2	1 Cauac	Dec 1	1 Akb'al
Dec 15	1 Eb	Dec 14	1 Cib
Dec 28	1 Chicchan	Dec 27	1 Muluc

GREGORIAN	MAYAN	GREGORIAN	MAYAN
DATE	DATE	DATE	DATE

2006

Jan 9	1 Ik'
Jan 22	1 Men
Feb 4	1 Lamat
Feb 17	1 Imix

Feb 23–Mayan Year 7 Manik'

Mar 2	1 Ix
Mar 15	1 Manik'
Mar 28	1 Ahau
Apr 10	1 Ben
Apr 23	1 Cimi
May 6	1 Cauac
May 19	1 Eb
Jun 1	1 Chicchan
Jun 14	1 Etznab
Jun 27	1 Chuen
Jul 10	1 Kan
Jul 23	1 Caban
Aug 5	1 Oc
Aug 18	1 Akb'al
Aug 31	1 Cib
Sep 13	1 Muluc
Sep 26	1 Ik'
Oct 9	1 Men
Oct 22	1 Lamat
Nov 4	1 Imix
Nov 17	1 Ix
Nov 30	1 Manik'
Dec 13	1 Ahau
Dec 26	1 Ben

2007

Jan 8	1 Cimi
Jan 21	1 Cauac
Feb 3	1 Eb
Feb 16	1 Chicchan

Feb 23–Mayan Year 8 Eb

Mar 1	1 Etznab
Mar 14	1 Chuen
Mar 27	1 Kan
Apr 9	1 Caban
Apr 22	1 Oc
May 5	1 Akb'al
May 18	1 Cib
May 31	1 Muluc
Jun 13	1 Ik'
Jun 26	1 Men
Jul 9	1 Lamat
Jul 22	1 Imix
Aug 4	1 Ix
Aug 17	1 Manik'
Aug 30	1 Ahau
Sep 12	1 Ben
Sep 25	1 Cimi
Oct 8	1 Cauac
Oct 21	1 Eb
Nov 3	1 Chicchan
Nov 16	1 Etznab
Nov 29	1 Chuen
Dec 12	1 Kan
Dec 25	1 Caban

GREGORIAN DATE	MAYAN DATE	GREGORIAN DATE	MAYAN DATE
*2008		**2009**	
Jan 7	1 Oc	Jan 5	1 Ix
Jan 20	1 Akb'al	Jan 18	1 Manik'
Feb 2	1 Cib	Jan 31	1 Ahau
Feb 15	1 Muluc	Feb 13	1 Ben
Feb 23—Mayan Year 9 Caban		**Feb 22—Mayan Year 10 Ik'**	
Feb 28	1 Ik'	Feb 26	1 Cimi
Mar 12	1 Men	Mar 11	1 Cauac
Mar 25	1 Lamat	Mar 24	1 Eb
Apr 7	1 Imix	Apr 6	1 Chicchan
Apr 20	1 Ix	Apr 19	1 Etznab
May 3	1 Manik'	May 2	1 Chuen
May 16	1 Ahau	May 15	1 Kan
May 29	1 Ben	May 28	1 Caban
Jun 11	1 Cimi	Jun 10	1 Oc
Jun 24	1 Cauac	Jun 23	1 Akb'al
Jul 7	1 Eb	Jul 6	1 Cib
Jul 20	1 Chicchan	Jul 19	1 Muluc
Aug 2	1 Etznab	Aug 1	1 Ik'
Aug 15	1 Chuen	Aug 14	1 Men
Aug 28	1 Kan	Aug 27	1 Lamat
Sep 10	1 Caban	Sep 9	1 Imix
Sep 23	1 Oc	Sep 22	1 Ix
Oct 6	1 Akb'al	Oct 5	1 Manik'
Oct 19	1 Cib	Oct 18	1 Ahau
Nov 1	1 Muluc	Oct 31	1 Ben
Nov 14	1 Ik'	Nov 13	1 Cimi
Nov 27	1 Men	Nov 26	1 Cauac
Dec 10	1 Lamat	Dec 9	1 Eb
Dec 23	1 Imix	Dec 22	1 Chicchan

GREGORIAN DATE	MAYAN DATE	GREGORIAN DATE	MAYAN DATE
2010		**2011**	
Jan 4	1 Etznab	Jan 3	1 Ik'
Jan 17	1 Chuen	Jan 16	1 Men
Jan 30	1 Kan	Jan 29	1 Lamat
Feb 12	1 Caban	Feb 11	1 Imix
Feb 22–Mayan Year 11 Manik'		**Feb 22–Mayan Year 12 Eb**	
Feb 25	1 Oc	Feb 24	1 Ix
Mar 10	1 Akb'al	Mar 9	1 Manik'
Mar 23	1 Cib	Mar 22	1 Ahau
Apr 5	1 Muluc	Apr 4	1 Ben
Apr 18	1 Ik'	Apr 17	1 Cimi
May 1	1 Men	Apr 30	1 Cauac
May 14	1 Lamat	May 13	1 Eb
May 27	1 Imix	May 26	1 Chicchan
Jun 9	1 Ix	Jun 8	1 Etznab
Jun 22	1 Manik'	Jun 21	1 Chuen
Jul 5	1 Ahau	Jul 4	1 Kan
Jul 18	1 Ben	Jul 17	1 Caban
Jul 31	1 Cimi	Jul 30	1 Oc
Aug 13	1 Cauac	Aug 12	1 Akb'al
Aug 26	1 Eb	Aug 25	1 Cib
Sep 8	1 Chicchan	Sep 7	1 Muluc
Sep 21	1 Etznab	Sep 20	1 Ik'
Oct 4	1 Chuen	Oct 3	1 Men
Oct 17	1 Kan	Oct 16	1 Lamat
Oct 30	1 Caban	Oct 29	1 Imix
Nov 12	1 Oc	Nov 11	1 Ix
Nov 25	1 Akb'al	Nov 24	1 Manik'
Dec 8	1 Cib	Dec 7	1 Ahau
Dec 21	1 Muluc	Dec 20	1 Ben

GREGORIAN DATE	MAYAN DATE	GREGORIAN DATE	MAYAN DATE
*2012		**2013**	
Jan 2	1 Cimi	Jan 13	1 Akb'al
Jan 15	1 Cauac	Jan 26	1 Cib
Jan 28	1 Eb	Feb 8	1 Muluc
Feb 10	1 Chicchan	**Feb 21–Mayan Year 1 Ik'**	
Feb 22–Mayan Year 13 Caban		Feb 21	1 Ik'
Feb 23	1 Etznab	Mar 6	1 Men
Mar 7	1 Chuen	Mar 19	1 Lamat
Mar 20	1 Kan	Apr 1	1 Imix
Apr 2	1 Caban	Apr 14	1 Ix
Apr 15	1 Oc	Apr 27	1 Manik'
Apr 28	1 Akb'al	May 10	1 Ahau
May 11	1 Cib	May 23	1 Ben
May 24	1 Muluc	Jun 5	1 Cimi
Jun 6	1 Ik'	Jun 18	1 Cauac
Jun 19	1 Men	Jul 1	1 Eb
Jul 2	1 Lamat	Jul 14	1 Chicchan
Jul 15	1 Imix	Jul 27	1 Etznab
Jul 28	1 Ix	Aug 9	1 Chuen
Aug 10	1 Manik'	Aug 22	1 Kan
Aug 23	1 Ahau	Sep 4	1 Caban
Sep 5	1 Ben	Sep 17	1 Oc
Sep 18	1 Cimi	Sep 30	1 Akb'al
Oct 1	1 Cauac	Oct 13	1 Cib
Oct 14	1 Eb	Oct 26	1 Muluc
Oct 27	1 Chicchan	Nov 8	1 Ik'
Nov 9	1 Etznab	Nov 21	1 Men
Nov 22	1 Chuen	Dec 4	1 Lamat
Dec 5	1 Kan	Dec 17	1 Imix
Dec 18	1 Caban	Dec 30	1 Ix
Dec 31	1 Oc		

GREGORIAN DATE	MAYAN DATE	GREGORIAN DATE	MAYAN DATE
2014		**2015**	
Jan 12	1 Manik'	Jan 11	1 Chuen
Jan 25	1 Ahau	Jan 24	1 Kan
Feb 7	1 Ben	Feb 6	1 Caban
Feb 20	1 Cimi	Feb 19	1 Oc
Feb 21–Mayan Year 2 Manik'		**Feb 21–Mayan Year 3 Eb**	
Mar 5	1 Cauac	Mar 4	1 Akb'al
Mar 18	1 Eb	Mar 17	1 Cib
Mar 31	1 Chicchan	Mar 30	1 Muluc
Apr 13	1 Etznab	Apr 12	1 Ik'
Apr 26	1 Chuen	Apr 25	1 Men
May 9	1 Kan	May 8	1 Lamat
May 22	1 Caban	May 21	1 Imix
Jun 4	1 Oc	Jun 3	1 Ix
Jun 17	1 Akb'al	Jun 16	1 Manik'
Jun 30	1 Cib	Jun 29	1 Ahau
Jul 13	1 Muluc	Jul 12	1 Ben
Jul 26	1 Ik'	Jul 25	1 Cimi
Aug 8	1 Men	Aug 7	1 Cauac
Aug 21	1 Lamat	Aug 20	1 Eb
Sep 3	1 Imix	Sep 2	1 Chicchan
Sep 16	1 Ix	Sep 15	1 Etznab
Sep 29	1 Manik'	Sep 28	1 Chuen
Oct 12	1 Ahau	Oct 11	1 Kan
Oct 25	1 Ben	Oct 24	1 Caban
Nov 7	1 Cimi	Nov 6	1 Oc
Nov 20	1 Cauac	Nov 19	1 Akb'al
Dec 3	1 Eb	Dec 2	1 Cib
Dec 16	1 Chicchan	Dec 15	1 Muluc
Dec 29	1 Etznab	Dec 28	1 Ik'

GREGORIAN DATE	MAYAN DATE	GREGORIAN DATE	MAYAN DATE
*2016		**2017**	
Jan 10	1 Men	Jan 8	1 Cauac
Jan 23	1 Lamat	Jan 21	1 Eb
Feb 5	1 Imix	Feb 3	1 Chicchan
Feb 18	1 Ix	Feb 16	1 Etznab
Feb 21–Mayan Year 4 Caban		**Feb 20–Mayan Year 5 Ik'**	
Mar 2	1 Manik'	Mar 1	1 Chuen
Mar 15	1 Ahau	Mar 14	1 Kan
Mar 28	1 Ben	Mar 27	1 Caban
Apr 10	1 Cimi	Apr 9	1 Oc
Apr 23	1 Cauac	Apr 22	1 Akb'al
May 6	1 Eb	May 5	1 Cib
May 19	1 Chicchan	May 18	1 Muluc
Jun 1	1 Etznab	May 31	1 Ik'
Jun 14	1 Chuen	Jun 13	1 Men
Jun 27	1 Kan	Jun 26	1 Lamat
Jul 10	1 Caban	Jul 9	1 Imix
Jul 23	1 Oc	Jul 22	1 Ix
Aug 5	1 Akb'al	Aug 4	1 Manik'
Aug 18	1 Cib	Aug 17	1 Ahau
Aug 31	1 Muluc	Aug 30	1 Ben
Sep 13	1 Ik'	Sep 12	1 Cimi
Sep 26	1 Men	Sep 25	1 Cauac
Oct 9	1 Lamat	Oct 8	1 Eb
Oct 22	1 Imix	Oct 21	1 Chicchan
Nov 4	1 Ix	Nov 3	1 Etznab
Nov 17	1 Manik'	Nov 16	1 Chuen
Nov 30	1 Ahau	Nov 29	1 Kan
Dec 13	1 Ben	Dec 12	1 Caban
Dec 26	1 Cimi	Dec 25	1 Oc

GREGORIAN DATE	MAYAN DATE	GREGORIAN DATE	MAYAN DATE
2018		**2019**	
Jan 7	1 Akb'al	Jan 6	1 Manik'
Jan 20	1 Cib	Jan 19	1 Ahau
Feb 2	1 Muluc	Feb 1	1 Ben
Feb 15	1 Ik'	Feb 14	1 Cimi
Feb 20–Mayan Year 6 Manik'		**Feb 20–Mayan Year 7 Eb**	
Feb 28	1 Men	Feb 27	1 Cauac
Mar 13	1 Lamat	Mar 12	1 Eb
Mar 26	1 Imix	Mar 25	1 Chicchan
Apr 8	1 Ix	Apr 7	1 Etznab
Apr 21	1 Manik'	Apr 20	1 Chuen
May 4	1 Ahau	May 3	1 Kan
May 17	1 Ben	May 16	1 Caban
May 30	1 Cimi	May 29	1 Oc
Jun 12	1 Cauac	Jun 11	1 Akb'al
Jun 25	1 Eb	Jun 24	1 Cib
Jul 8	1 Chicchan	Jul 7	1 Muluc
Jul 21	1 Etznab	Jul 20	1 Ik'
Aug 3	1 Chuen	Aug 2	1 Men
Aug 16	1 Kan	Aug 15	1 Lamat
Aug 29	1 Caban	Aug 28	1 Imix
Sep 11	1 Oc	Sep 10	1 Ix
Sep 24	1 Akb'al	Sep 23	1 Manik'
Oct 7	1 Cib	Oct 6	1 Ahau
Oct 20	1 Muluc	Oct 19	1 Ben
Nov 2	1 Ik'	Nov 1	1 Cimi
Nov 15	1 Men	Nov 14	1 Cauac
Nov 28	1 Lamat	Nov 27	1 Eb
Dec 11	1 Imix	Dec 10	1 Chicchan
Dec 24	1 Ix	Dec 23	1 Etznab

GREGORIAN DATE	MAYAN DATE

*2020

Jan 5	1 Chuen
Jan 18	1 Kan
Jan 31	1 Caban
Feb 13	1 Oc

Feb 20–Mayan Year 8 Caban

Feb 26	1 Akb'al
Mar 10	1 Cib
Mar 23	1 Muluc
Apr 5	1 Ik'
Apr 18	1 Men
May 1	1 Lamat
May 14	1 Imix
May 27	1 Ix
Jun 9	1 Manik'
Jun 22	1 Ahau
Jul 5	1 Ben
Jul 18	1 Cimi
Jul 31	1 Cauac
Aug 13	1 Eb
Aug 26	1 Chicchan
Sep 8	1 Etznab
Sep 21	1 Chuen
Oct 4	1 Kan
Oct 17	1 Caban
Oct 30	1 Oc
Nov 12	1 Akb'al
Nov 25	1 Cib
Dec 8	1 Muluc
Dec 21	1 Ik'

EXPLANATORY NOTES

On the title "The Serpent and the Jaguar."

It may not be surprising that the title of this book refers to two of the day signs of the Tzolk'in. But why the Serpent and why the Jaguar? Each and every day sign of the sacred calendar carries a profound meaning and its own special power, so how to choose one, or two, that can represent the essence of this book?

For me, it was never a matter of choice—there was simply never any question. The Jaguar, Ix, is the most enigmatic animal of the deep jungle, carrying the ancient secrets of timeless forests. It represents the vitality and spirit of life and all living things, and endows us with the spiritual and psychological strength required to attain the highest levels of consciousness. We need this vitality and strength as we seek to align our awareness and our lives with the rhythms of the Tzolk'in.

The Serpent, Chicchan, is one of the most powerful day signs in the Tzolk'in. It represents transcendence and the transformation of time and knowledge into wisdom, but is also the lord of all material things and the nagual of education. What better day sign to shepherd us along our quest to learn about and transform our relationship with sacred, cyclical time, and intertwine the Tzolk'in with our physical and material lives?

This is why it felt natural that the Serpent and the Jaguar would be our guides for this journey into the Tzolk'in.

On the uniqueness of this book.

The shelves of my library hold the names of many well-known and respected authors in the Mayan world: Linda Schele, Carlos Barrios, Ken Johnson, Dr. Robert Sitler, Gaspar Pedro González, Dr. Mark Van Stone, Dr. Carl Johan Calleman, John Major Jenkins, Bruce Scofield, and Daniel Pinchbeck, among others. Each and every one of these authors has illuminated one more stepping stone in my journey to know the Mayan Calendar and the profoundly ancient culture it comes from, and for that I am thankful.

Yet the one thing I had always searched for throughout my studies of the Tzolk'in and its application to everyday life, was missing. No book existed—that I could find—that interpreted the entire cycle of 260 days—either in general or within the specific context of the modern world. Most books on Mayan astrology or the calendar provide the descriptions of the day signs and the numbers, and explain, in greater or lesser detail, how the Tzolk'in works, how to calculate your Mayan birthsign or your Mayan cross (the full birth chart), and so on. But the real benefit of the Tzolk'in, as far as daily life is concerned, lies in that special combination of the number and the day sign and their complementary energies, blended and interpreted within the specific context of the environment in which you live.

One way to gain access to these daily energies is to put up a Maya Daykeeper in your house. This, of course, is not too practical for most of us. Another is to travel to Guatemala and spend a Tzolk'in round or two with the Maya Daykeepers. Also not practical. A third way is to take the time to learn how to do it yourself. And so, I was left with the only option faced by all writers when they can't find the book they seek: write it.

On the origin of the word "Tzolk'in."

As Mayan scholar and author Ken Johnson recounted to me during one of our many conversations, the word "tzolk'in" was never really used by the Maya to refer to their sacred calendar. In the early 20th century, Western scholars studying the Mayan civilization were using Yucatec as the Maya language of choice, but the Yucatec Maya had stopped using the Calendar sometime in the latter half of the 19th century. The scholars tried to come up with a term for the 260-day sacred calendar, because, in Ken's words, "they didn't have the vaguest idea what it was called by the Classic Maya. One of them (can't remember who), had spent time in the highlands of Guatemala, and said, 'The K'iche' call it *ch'ol q'ij*, and in Yucatec that would be *tzolk'in*, so why don't we call it that?' "

And so they did. In K'iche' Maya, *ch'ol* means "count" and *q'ij* means "day"—in other words, "count of days." In Yucatec Maya, the equivalent terms are *tzol* and *k'in*. Ken adds that the K'iche' term *ch'ol q'ij* is in fact an abbreviated rendering of the more accurate *ch'ol b'al q'ij*.

Curiously, recently epigraphers have been coming across a term which they read as "*saq haab*," which would be translated as "white year" or "sacred year," if we are to take the word "white" in its other meanings of "heavenly" or "sacred." Some epigraphers believe that this may be the Classic Period name for the Tzolk'in.

There is also some debate regarding capitalization of the word "Tzolk'in." While most academic books do not capitalize it, the contemporary Maya do. I have decided to follow the practice of the Maya, out of deference and respect to them and this ancient calendar. It should be noted, additionally, that Allen Christenson's dictionary of the K'iche' language does have the equivalent K'iche' term capitalized as *Ch'ol Q'ij*. Jean Molesky-Poz of Santa Clara University also capitalizes *Ch'ol Q'ij* in her work.

On the first day sign.

You will notice this book begins the cycle of trecenas and the 260 daily energies of the Tzolk'in with the day sign Caban, not Imix as so many of us are used to. While this may be a point of some surprise, contention, or resistance to change, the fact remains that Imix is not considered to be the first day sign of the Tzolk'in by most, if not all, Maya peoples.

The K'iche' Maya, as Don Rigoberto Itzep Chanchavac personally confirmed to me, consider Caban to be the first day sign—if you really need a "first" day sign, that is. By its nature, the Tzolk'in is a cyclical calendar; as such, it really has no "first" or "last" day sign. There is no beginning and there is no end. The 20 day signs and the 13 numbers that comprise its structure interlock in an endless dance of 260 combinations per cycle.

Imagine coming in for a landing on Planet Earth. Our planet is a sphere, the three-dimensional version of the circle. Your co-pilot says, "Let's enter at the first place on Earth." You'd be a bit hard-pressed to find the "first place" on a round planet. The same concept applies to the Tzolk'in, the four-dimensional version of the circle. You can "enter," or begin living with, the sacred calendar at any point, at any time.

It is our linearly oriented consciousness that tends to demand a beginning and an end to anything having to do with time. However, since this is a book, with a defined beginning and end, we need to start somewhere, and so I have chosen Caban, the day sign that the K'iche' Maya consider to be the first.

And for those of you who are just not satisfied with that... yes, popular convention says that the start of the Tzolk'in is 1 Imix. Unfortunately, no matter how much you may have gotten used to Imix as the start of the Tzolk'in, this is simply not true. The Aztecs did indeed begin *their* calendar count on 1 Imix, and many in the West, including author Dr. Carl Calleman, have adopted that practice. We do not know for sure which day served as the first day of the Tzolk'in in the times of the Classic Maya; in modern times, the first day varies from Maya clan to Maya clan.

The Yucatec Maya, who stopped using the Calendar altogether about 150 years ago, started their count with Kan (K'at). The people of Lake Atitlan count from Men (Tz'ikin), the Kaqchikel Maya begin with 1 Chuen (B'atz'), and the Mam Maya of the Cuchumatanes Mountains prefer to begin with 9 Eb (E'). The K'iche' Maya, whose calendar tradition is considered widely by scholars to be the closest to ancient or Classical Maya practices, celebrate the Tzolk'in "New Year" on 8 B'atz' ("Chuen" in Yucatec).

There is, however, no concrete evidence that the ancient Maya used 1 Imix as the first day of a new 260-day cycle. None of the living Maya, it seems, start on an Imix day because it is an unpredictable and volatile day. In fact, the Maya avoid doing much of anything at all on Imix days.

On the Use of Yucatec and K'iche'.

There are approximately 30 Maya languages currently in use today; in the Classic Period, scholars believe there were only two primary linguistic branches: Yucatec and Cholan. This book lists the terminologies of the Tzolk'in in both Yucatec and K'iche', the two most well-known Maya languages in as well as outside Central

America. Each number, day sign and energy of the day description
list first the Yucatec and then the K'iche' version of the numbers and
day signs. For example:

Ho (5) Lamat (Yucatec Maya)
Job' (5) Q'anil (K'iche' Maya)

Purely for reasons of popular familiarity, I have selected the Yucatec
versions of the numbers and day signs as the primary language of
reference in the Trecena descriptions and the Energies of the Day. I
do however strongly urge you to become familiar with the K'iche'
terminology as well, because it can expand your access to and
understanding of the sacred calendar significantly.

RESOURCES

BOOKS

13 B'aktun—Mayan Visions of 2012 and Beyond
Gaspar Pedro González

2012: Science and Prophecy of the Ancient Maya
Mark Van Stone, PhD

The Ancient Spirituality of the Modern Maya
Thomas Hart

The Book of Destiny: Unlocking the Secrets of the Ancient Maya
Carlos Barrios

Breaking the Maya Code
Michael D. Coe

Contemporary Maya Spirituality: The Ancient Ways Are Not Lost
Jean Molesky-Poz

How to Read Maya Hieroglyphs
John Montgomery

Jaguar Wisdom: an Introduction to the Mayan Calendar
Kenneth Johnson

The Living Maya: Ancient Wisdom in the Era of 2012
Robert Sitler, PhD

Maya 2012: A Guide to Celebrations in Mexico, Guatemala, Belize & Honduras
Joshua Berman

Mayan Calendar Astrology: Mapping Your Inner Cosmos
Kenneth Johnson

The Mayan Calendar and the Transformation of Consciousness
Carl Johan Calleman, PhD

Maya Cosmos: Three Thousand Years on the Shaman's Path
David Freidel, Linda Schele, and Joy Parker

Popol Vuh: The Definitive Edition of the Mayan Book of the Dawn of Life and the Glories of Gods and Kings
Dennis Tedlock

Secrets of the Talking Jaguar
Martin Prechtel

Time and the Highland Maya
Barbara Tedlock

MOBILE APPS

MCP Mayan Tzolkin (iPhone and Android)
Get your Tzolk'in Energy of the Day reading, plus descriptions of the day signs, numbers, and deities. This is the award-winning official mobile app of the Mayan Calendar Portal.

My Mayan Match (iPhone and Android)
Discover the nature of your compatibility with the people in your life. This app is based on the little-known personal compatibility matrix embedded in the sacred Tzolk'in calendar.

WEB SITES

European Association of Mayanists: **www.wayeb.com**

Foundation for the Advancement of Mesoamerican Studies: **www.famsi.org**

Jaguar Wisdom: **www.jaguarwisdom.org**

Mayan Calendar Portal: **www.maya-portal.net** and **www.facebook.com/mayancalendarportal**

Mayan Majix: **www.mayanmajix.com**

The Mesoamerica Center: **www.utmesoamerica.org**

Mesoweb: **www.mesoweb.com**

Mundo Maya online: **www.mayadiscovery.com**

ON A PERSONAL NOTE

I wrote this book for all those of you who seek to enhance your daily lives with the energies and rhythms of the sacred Tzolk'in, and who seek to know the nature of Sacred Time. Living with both sacred and secular time isn't easy in modern Western society; our lives are on a constant schedule, rolling deadlines, to-do lists, obligations, responsibilities. There never seems to be enough time to do the things we have to do, let alone time to just be.

But the Tzolk'in allows us to step out of the race and the stress, and turn at least a few moments of each day into sacred time. Each time you meditate, every moment you take to honor the dawn as it slips over the hills (or the building across the street), to appreciate the food you are about to eat, or to laugh with your children, every breath you take in quiet awareness of your worth and your potential, is a piece of sacred time.

I stand humbled by the impact of the Energies of the Day on the lives of so many, all those of you who have commented and shared your reaction to these energies that are printed in this book, in our app, and that we post on our Facebook page. That is high confirmation for me that the Tzolk'in truly does work, and resonate with the human spirit.

Where do the descriptions of these energies come from? Perhaps it's a poet's inspiration. Or a connection with that divine collective consciousness where all intuition, knowledge, and art come from. The Mayan Calendar has a way of bringing out more than just art—it connects us all no matter where or who we are, Maya or non Maya.

I hope you enjoy this book as much as I have enjoyed writing it, and that it brings another ray of light to your life's path. And if you are so moved as to send me your comments or questions, I would be honored to receive them via email at info@maya-portal.net.

Namaste, mal tyox, dyos bo'otik, and in lak'ech.

About the Author

Writer, poet, producer, entrepreneur, Birgitte Rasine serves as the Chief Evolution Officer (CEO) of LUCITÀ Inc., a hybrid design and communications firm committed, in its work and practices, to sustainability. She is also the producer of the well-known Mayan Calendar Portal (www.maya-portal.net and www.facebook.com/mayancalendarportal), aka the MCP, the leading portal web site dedicated to the sacred Mayan Calendar. Ms. Rasine has produced numerous webinars and interview sessions on the Mayan Calendar and Mayan astrology, presenting to MCP audiences such experts and scholars as Kenneth Johnson, Dr. Robert Sitler, Maya author Gaspar Pedro González, Dr. Carl Calleman, and Nobel Peace Prize laureate Rigoberta Menchú Tum.

The unique perspective Ms. Rasine brings to this interpretation of the days of the Tzolk'in comes from her vast and varied life and professional experience. She has lived in six countries and speaks five languages. She has interacted with people from all walks of life, from media and business professionals to environmental activists and government officials from all over the world, from artists and musicians to families and children in developing countries. She has worked as a journalist, screenwriter, playwright, PR executive, marketing professional, non profit representative, and high tech copywriter, writing and editing materials as diverse as independent Hollywood screenplays, articles about the international film industry, funding proposals for NASA's Martian exploration technologies, documentation for cyber security systems, and materials for the energy, health & wellness, and food & beverage sectors, to name just a few. She has also traveled to the lands of the Maya, swum in ancient Maya waterways, spoken with modern-day Maya about their lives, and peered directly into the blue abyss of a cenoté. As a journalist, she has the skill of observation, analysis, and description without a personal agenda; as a researcher, she is tireless in confirming information and tracking down sources; as a poet, she has the gift of song through words.

A prolific photographer and award-winning poet, Ms. Rasine holds a BA in Aesthetics of Film from Stanford University, studied cinematography at the American Film Institute in Los Angeles, California, and completed a professional masters program in international relations at the Instituto Universitario Ortega y Gasset in Madrid, Spain. She sits on the board of directors of a Czech and Slovak non profit organization in New York City dedicated to supporting the leaders of tomorrow, and is a member of several professional organizations including the Association of Women in Water, Energy and the Environment.

Connect with Birgitte:

Web
www.birgitterasine.com

Twitter
twitter.com/birgitte_rasine

Goodreads
www.goodreads.com/birgitte_rasine

Pinterest
pinterest.com/birgitterasine

Facebook
www.facebook.com/birgitterasine

Google Plus
https://plus.google.com/u/0/+BirgitteRasine

DISCLAIMER

The Mayan world is not like our modern, industrialized, "developed" world. We like to have everything served to us according to standards of quality, consistency, predictability. In the lands of the Maya, life is a bit more organic.

Not all Daykeepers agree on all aspects of the Tzolk'in, or Mayan astrology in general. Practices, interpretations, and rituals may vary from place to place. Then there are all those web sites and books and videos that claim to have "the truth" about the Maya and their Calendar. To make matters more challenging still, much of the knowledge and records of the ancient Maya about their extraordinary calendar, astronomy, science, and other parts of their culture has been, as we know, ruthlessly destroyed, erased off the face of the planet by visionless, fanatical *conquistadores* driven by power and greed. The "discovery" of the Americas was followed by centuries of destruction, savagery, and oppression. Today, many Maya remain cut off from their own cultural roots, living in Spanish-speaking cities and towns. But many of those same Maya are also now starting to return to the villages to re-learn the Calendar and its practice, and to reconnect with their roots.

The information presented in this book is based on extensive research along with countless conversations and emails with the Maya scholars mentioned in the Acknowledgments and Maya elder Don Rigoberto Itzep Chanchavac from the highlands of Guatemala. I have taken great pains to gather the most authentic descriptions of the day signs and the numbers possible in order to express the meaning of the energies embodied in each of the Tzolk'in's 260 days, as they apply to the realities of our modern society. The "Energies of the Day" section of this book are my personal interpretation of these energies; others may express them differently. These are the same energy texts that have resonated so profoundly with thousands of people around the world who are a part of the vast Mayan Calendar

Portal community; many have written in to say how their lives have changed as a result of following these energies. While neither I nor my publisher can guarantee specific results or outcomes with any of the content of this book, the energies have indeed had an impact on many in our international community, as evidenced by their direct, proactive comments and feedback.

This is the beauty and accessibility of this sacred calendar: each one of us can interpret the energies and the days according to our own spiritual and emotional sensibilities and needs. Indeed, if we were all to write our own version of this book, there would be 6.978 billion editions! In this way, the Tzolk'in truly becomes a personal guide, a powerful horizon toward which to orient your life path.

I do not claim that every word in this book is incontrovertible fact; all authors writing about ancient cultures should always be open to the possibility of new discoveries that may throw some or all of a certain body of knowledge into question. In fact, this book itself is a living document—as new information comes to light, we will be able to produce revised editions.

What I *can* say is that I have done my best in bringing to you what I consider to be an unbiased, unadulterated presentation of the sacred Tzolk'in calendar and an interpretation of its energies specifically intended for people living in modern industrialized society. It is my hope that this is the way in which this book is received and utilized.